Glimpses of the Life and Work of
G.D. WATSON

Glimpses of the Life and Work of

G.D. WATSON

By His Wife, Eva M. Watson

Kingsley Press

Shoals, Indiana

Glimpses of the Life and Work of G. D. Watson

Published by Kingsley Press
PO Box 973
Shoals, IN 47581
USA

Tel. (800) 971-7985
www.kingsleypress.com
E-mail: sales@kingsleypress.com

ISBN: 978-1-937428-90-7 (Paperback)

ISBN: 978-1-937428-91-4 (E-Book)

Dedication

To his friends and their families and those among whom he ministered, this volume is affectionately dedicated.

Contents

Foreword

THIS little book has long been on my mind, but it is late appearing. We must believe this is God's time for it, and we cheerfully accept his ruling. Every step of the way has been in much prayer for his leading.

We are indebted to Dr. Levin P. Causey for the first chapter. He was a schoolmate and closely associated with Dr. Watson in his youthful years, and their friendship was never broken. He knew him possibly as no other man ever did, and we appreciate his words.

Evangelist J. M. Hames has written the chapter, "A Man sent from God," which I highly appreciate, and I know the readers will.

Rev. Will Huff was a helper in advice, which has been a great blessing.

Many encouraging words from various directions have enabled me to complete the work. It has been penned with mine own hand and without the aid of a secretary as a loving tribute to my husband's memory.

> *And now I am flinging this recklessly out*
> *Like a chip on the stream of the Infinite will*
> *And I just let my God His great purpose fulfill.*

Eva M. Watson

Preface

Memories from Our Children

Years ago, when I was quite a small girl, I remember one day my father and I were taking a walk. One thing he said has stayed with me down the years. It was this: "Your mind is like a room with shelves around the wall. The things you remember are like packages which you lay on the shelves. They are living packages like fairies, and don't always wait to be called. Sometimes they will jump off the shelf and come to you unbidden. At other times they seem to run and hide, but they are there; and if you call and hunt, they come running out."

Now that the time has come when I no longer can see that loved face or hear the dear voice, many memories come trooping forth from memory's room.

I could not have been more than three years old when I remember often stealing quietly into his study where he sat writing sermons. He was busy, but I was not turned away. The big old dictionary was laid on the floor; and for as long as I wished I might sit by it, studying the many pictures and whispering to myself. A year or so later when my small brother was old enough to play, Papa would delight us by crawling around on his hands and knees pretending to be a bear or a lion according to our orders. His growls and roars seemed so realistic that we would grow hysterical in our shouts and attempts to escape the clutches of the wild animal. He often brought home candy in his pocket; and he would come in saying, "I've got catch meddlers in my pocket." This meant he could be bombarded with questions and hunting until we found what it was the meddlers would find. That was always his expression at Christmas time, only then we might not know until Christmas morning what all the bundles he was loaded with contained.

Ah, those Christmases! The tree and the presents and the stockings! After they were all examined and admired, we sat quietly in a circle while he read the sweet old story of the babe in the manger. Then, while we all knelt, he would pour out his heart in a wonderful prayer. Yes, he loved Christmas. Even the last one he spent on earth he was so pleased with his simple gifts; and though suffering the ravages of disease, he was able to repeat almost the entire poem of Milton's "Hymn of the Nativity."

Just a few hours before he left us, he asked me to sing; and I sang the best I could, "When the mists have rolled in splendor."

The last time I heard his wonderful voice raised in song was just three weeks before he died. He sang, "When we all get to heaven, what a meeting that will be!" He was a wonderful traveling companion. The Iron Horse was a real one to us children, as he would tell us what the different whistles meant; for he knew all the signals. When he could no longer travel, the tears would trickle down his face as he would listen to the train whistle and say, "My traveling days in this world are over."

I loved to hear him preach. His sermons always sounded new to me. And the happy days spent as a family traveling through the South while he and my mother held meetings! I shall never forget those days. The little Florida town where the weekly prayer meeting was held in our home, and the tiny chapel he built for the town, are blessed memories.

The grandchildren called him "Gaga," a name given him by my first wee daughter. He never came empty handed. There was always a penny or some little gift for each child. He loved to do things for others more than anyone I ever saw, but it was hard for him to be helpless while others did things for him.

On that last while I watched the failing breath and knew that those piercing eyes could no longer see me, I was glad his going was so quiet and gentle. To me it was as a great ship, which, having sailed many seas and weathered many gales, comes into harbor. The masts and spars are worn and the sails are furled. Gently and silently she glides from the turbulent sea into the quiet harbor, slowly approaches the great pier and touches it so smoothly that it is hard to tell when it docks. Thus it was with him. One last gentle sigh and life's voyage was over. He was safe home at last.

—Luella Watson Kinder

Men are like mountains; you have to get a distance away to appreciate their magnitude. After a few short years, I find that I miss my father more even than at first. Looking back towards the days when he was with us, he stands higher now than I saw him then. Every life has certain individual moods that stamp it. In thinking of him, this, his preacher son, naturally recalls those items of his ministerial life and work. Of these the following especially impressed me!

First, his absolute sincerity. He was a man who believed. In a day of so much doubt and when so many seem hardly to know what they believe, if anything, it was refreshing to make contact with one who had no doubts in spiritual matters. The next thing to stand out in my memory of him was his fearlessness. He never was afraid to speak out his convictions. This also is a trait not found in very many today in public life. Evil had to face the bar of justice in his sermons. Wrong had no flimsy mask to hide behind, but came forth to face justice in his messages. Thirdly, I think of him as one who had the ability to inspire others. He was a born leader. Had he entered politics, he would have risen high as a leader of men. As a preacher, he rose higher as a leader of human souls. People who were timid, doubting, and afraid, after meeting him, went away feeling they had a rock to stand upon. He put heart into folks.

One of the last if not his very last words ever spoken to me were, "Preach the gospel." Having fought the good fight, he was ready to pass on, but he wanted someone else—yes, many others—to "carry on." We who knew him face this challenge. May God help us to meet it!

—Rev. Fletcher G. Watson

In my experience in the world of business, and as a member of the state legislature and in the practice of law, I have come in contact with a number of prominent men. I have met persons, many famous speakers, and have broken bread with a large number of keen and brilliant wits; but I have never met a man whose mind was more active, alert, and as keen as my father's. He was a born storyteller and thoroughly enjoyed a sharp, keen encounter with learned men and women.

About thirty years ago, when the negro dialect stories of Joel Chandler Harris came out, my father purchased one of his first books for me; and I never will forget sitting on the wide veranda of our rambling home in Windsor, Florida, with the air heavy with southern odors of fruit and field, how my father would delight in settling himself down in a comfortable rocking chair, with a tray close by heaped up with delicious oranges or other fruit, and reading aloud the stories from this book. He was quite a mimic, and his facial expression was a delight to one who enjoyed the folklore stories of the South. Being raised in the South himself, he could readily express the negro dialect and would make gesticulations with his right hand while holding the book with his left. He would read again and again the quaint stories of Uncle Remus.

He was also apt and impelling as a story teller, and we never grew weary of hearing him recount his past experiences as a young boy, then in his early manhood and later his different experiences in the ministry. He had a wonderful memory for names and faces. As I have been out with him at many camp meetings, it was always marvelous to me how he could remember and recollect numerous people who had met him in former years, calling them by name and stating the time and place where they had met and recalling instances of their associations.

He also possessed a very fine musical voice, and many evenings were pleasantly spent in singing the old time negro melodies on our porch; and later in the evening, when assembled for family worship, he would always lead in his strong voice the hymns of Zion. Among his favorite songs were: "Oh Thou in Whose Presence My Soul Takes Delight," "My Jesus, I Love Thee," "How Firm a Foundation," and "Blessed Assurance." At

New Year's we always sang the New Year song, "Come, Let Us Anew." His favorite negro melody was "Roll, Jordan, Roll." Many years ago when he was holding revival services in Lorraine, Ohio, I, at that time being located in Cleveland, went down one Saturday night to be with him over Sunday. The people desired to hear some of the negro songs, and he called me to the pulpit with him and we sang many of his favorites, which greatly delighted the congregation.

Living in Florida and resting from his work in the winter, he would improve his time by reading many spiritual books, as well as keeping up with the times by having the best magazines and papers at hand. He was greatly interested in the arts and sciences and was a firm believer in the Constitution of the United States, as well as the development of our national resources and modern inventions. He could talk with clearness and authority upon almost any subject of national importance. His mind was a veritable storehouse of knowledge and information. He loved poetry and could recite page after page from Young's "Night Thoughts," "Paradise Lost," and the works of Longfellow, Whittier, Tennyson, and others. Among his favorite poems was that of Longfellow's "The Bridge," commencing, "I stood on the bridge at midnight and the clock was striking the hour," which poem has been put to music and which he dearly loved to sing. He was always a seeker of knowledge and greatly enjoyed literary and scientific articles. Needless to say, the deeper and more spiritual books and articles were devoured by him. The works of Faber and Madame Guyon were of never failing interest to him.

—George C. Watson

CHAPTER 1

Resume

EUROPE did a fine piece of work for America and the world when it sent some of its virile stock to settle and populate the Cape Charles Peninsula. Many are the sons and daughters of note that have risen to do honor to the sires and dames of these pioneers. To name only a few of those who have become famous is to suggest many others who may not be named. Among the truly great Eastern shoremen may be mentioned Robert Lawrence Dashiell, George Alfred Townsend, Henry A. Wise, E. King Wilson, Robert Laird Collier, John Walter Smith, Howard W. Selby. In George Douglas Watson the old peninsula has produced one man difficult, if not impossible, of classification. He stands apart, unique, a rare genius. He was no copyist. His chariot wheels were not loaded with and stirred up by other drivers. His thinking was Watsonian, of the George type. His rhetoric was according to the rules of Watson. He was largely self-trained, and it would have been difficult to train him otherwise. He was original to an unusual degree, not that he ignored entirely the thoughts and works of others. This may no man do. He read voraciously and absorbed what he read, but he had the power of transforming and resetting that which he gathered from others, until it stood forth clothed in new dress and bearing the image of originality. Like the plants, absorbing from the earth and air, the elements suited to their respective lives, and reproducing them in entirely new forms, so Watson collected from his reading and other mingling with the thought and life of society, the elements of thought and life suited to his individuality, digested and absorbed the same, and reproduced them in rare new forms that sparkled and gloried with the brilliance of his own inimitable style.

In the life of George Watson were mingled rare natural endowments and hard work. He excelled both as a speaker and a writer. In his early pastorates in the Wilmington Conference, his sermons foretold the coming pulpit paragon. Treading, as he did, in the steps of some of the great preachers of that day, he was recognized by the cultivated laymen who heard him as a new light in thought and sermonic expression.

Great preachers who heard him and read his writings were impressed that a star of great magnitude had risen among them. Dr. Robert N. Baer, of the Baltimore Conference, said of him, when he had been preaching only some half dozen years, that no other man could say things as Watson said them. He was soon found in charge of that brainy church in Dover, Delaware; and by that time his ability was so well known that, at the suggestion of that great preacher, Dr. R. L. Dashiell, he was transferred to Indianapolis and stationed at the great Meridian Street Church.

It must not be thought that Dr. Watson, because of his rare talent and great achievements, was devoid of the ordinary characteristics of men. He was very much alive in the domestic and social relations of life. His home and his family held large place in his heart. His friends ever found in him a loyal and helpful brother. He was generous almost to a fault. While conscious of possessing talent and power, he was ever appreciative of the gifts and work of others. He was warmly affectionate in his nature, and lavishly poured out the ardor of his soul upon those he loved. His temperament was intense. He thought, labored, and loved intensely.

While only a boy in his teens, George Watson enlisted in the Confederate Army and served three years as a soldier. At the close of the war, being then only twenty years old, he saw the folly of the rebellion and, like many other Southern youths, changed his politics.

While in the army, under the influence of a Southern Methodist chaplain, he was converted. Upon his return home to Onancock, Virginia, he joined the Methodist Episcopal Church.

Later he studied at the Methodist General Biblical Institute at Concord, New Hampshire.

Not many of the Concord students of those days, and none of the professors, are living. But through a series of years there were those who remembered with appreciation the bright, impetuous Virginia boy who, from time to time, enlivened the debates and stirred the prayer meetings in the halls of the old institute building.

Religiously, Dr. Watson was orthodox and very devout. His experience was positive and clear. As years advanced, his maturing thought led him to a very deep consecration, resulting in a very profound consciousness of spiritual holiness. The more mature years of his ministry were given to teaching the doctrine and leading others into the experience of this high state of grace.

To his gift in speaking and writing, Dr. Watson added that of song. His commanding voice in the leadership of praise, at camp meetings and other religious services, is still recalled by some who heard him in his early ministry.

Dr. Watson's great capacity for labor is illustrated by his last evangelistic effort. A several months' engagement, when he was at the age of seventy-six, took him across the States, from the Carolinas into Canada, preaching twice daily much of the time. He kept up the pace for a few months,when he collapsed with diabetes, and returned to his home to end his career in three years of wasting decline.

This reference is made here only to show the great energy which characterized his entire ministry. The subject of his life and work will be more fully treated in later chapters of this book.

CHAPTER 2

Conversion

WE have very little data, a few notes, and memory from which we may be able to give a few glimpses into the life and work of this man to his many friends. Those who knew him best in later years knew nothing of his early life with its aspirations and struggles.

He set his mark and, like the ocean liner, determined to reach it, although rough winds and waves intervened. Shall we let all the lessons be lost, that might be given to future generations, or shall we cull out a few for those who may profit by reading them?

The latter is the aim of this writing. Not many mighty are called, not many of the great ones of earth, but the willing mind and humble heart in God's hand are the requisites for accomplishing some mighty tasks for him. Truly, he was a chosen vessel for this work, to which he felt called so early in life.

Having a sympathetic nature, he shared the sorrows of others and often made them his own. At a time when receiving only eight hundred dollars a year for his services and having a family of three to support, he was told that a poor brother would lose a hundred dollars because a friend could not pay his debt for that amount. George sold his horse and gave the amount to pay the debt. The Lord had opened the way for him in another pastorate where he needed no horse.

Being humble minded, he was easily approached. The poorest person or the lowliest would not be abashed to come to him for counsel or help.

He had a goodly heritage from his parents. It was the best. They were thrifty, but not rich in this world's goods.

His father, James Henderson Watson, descended from a family who, from time immemorial, were tillers of the soil. They were, and continue to be, noted for integrity, sobriety, and unwavering religious principles.

James was one of eleven children, all of whom grew to maturity. All were well trained and stood high in the community in which they lived. They were strictly temperate, and brought up their families the same. They were true to the Sunday school and church of their choice, which was the Methodist Episcopal.

James was a quiet, self-possessed man, gentle and undemonstrative, but strong in purpose.

The mother, Mary Emeline Scarburgh Watson, who came of an Episcopalian family, was equal to her husband in strength of character. She would have been termed a "live wire" in these days.

A mother of six boys, she needed and possessed alertness and great wisdom as well as firmness. Her family of Scarburghs, for generations back, have revealed choice and ability for military and professional careers.

We do not wonder that three of her own sons volunteered to give their services, and two gave their lives to the Civil War. When God took her to himself, leaving her boys in childhood, the people said, "How sad that she must die and leave these boys—they need her kind of training."

In his great mercy God took the infant son a month in advance of the mother's death, and the little four-year-old, Alfred, died on the same day she passed away.

George Douglas was the third son. He received a loving welcome on March 23, 1845, into the family circle. The home was a modest farmhouse such as were built in those days on the eastern shore of Accomac County, Virginia, but the hearts were large.

No one sought his name for the cradle roll, as at the present day, but he was dedicated to God in baptism; and the parents sought to live up to all their promises.

Very early in life the parents took the little ones to church services. When only a few years old, George climbed upon a box and tried to repeat what the preacher had said the previous Sunday, to his little playmates around him.

He was ten years of age when bereft of his mother. He greatly missed her motherly care and restraint and, as he grew older, became restive and unhappy. He also desired to study, more than anything else, for he was a student from earliest childhood. When he had not teachers or books, he studied nature. He possessed a very serious turn of mind, with a strain of sadness that ran through all his life. With a vivid imagination he was naturally easily elated and as easily depressed. In his childhood his were wonderful daydreams, and some of them came true.

At that date the Sunday blue laws were practiced in that part of the country.

Also slavery, in its mildest form, prevailed here. Although his father had no slaves, it was the custom for farmers who owned none to hire them by the year from those who had more than they needed for their own farms. These slaves must have their day of rest, and it was accorded to them as theirs, except for doing chores. It was from these that George first heard of old folklore. They delighted to tell how "old brer rabbit" always came out ahead of all other animals. The white children enjoyed clustering around the hero who could tell this best. Joel Chandler Harris depicts it very correctly.

The Sabbaths were broken into by an occasional visitor sometimes.

There were no moving pictures to entice the children and young people from the house of God and no automobiles to insure a speedy transit to some remote region where crowds had assembled. Hence the quiet Sabbath, with its rest, was left for church services; and the children of Christian parents were expected to attend with them and quietly listen to the preacher. Of course, they took naps, but that was in order since the services were sufficiently long to admit of such rest in between the divisions of the discourse. Their youthful minds were plastic; and without much, if any, effort they received good impressions, and a foundation was laid that was durable. There were no young people's meetings to be a benefit.

George was a leader among his associates. He soon learned to sing and was quite pleased when, before he was half grown, he could help to pitch and lead the tunes in meeting. He was an apt scholar and possessed a good memory which served him well all his life. Once when very small he had been reprimanded for some misconduct, and he stopped crying, and said, "I know, I've got to preach the everlasting gospel." This call went with him all through the years of his boyhood, even while rejecting the call, "Son, give me thine heart."

The stepmother, a good, godly woman, sympathized with George in his tastes and appreciated all his boyish efforts. She was also a restraint to his youthful indiscretions and endeavored to guide him right. She and his father prayed much for George and longed to see him make God his choice. He was sent to the common school and soon absorbed all there was for him there.

About this time the family made a change, moving from Ames' Ridge to farther up the county, and located on Mt. Prospect farm. The very commodious farmhouse was built on the Onancock Creek, having the town of the same name just across on the opposite side. This was a fine location, commanding a view of the stream and the boats as they passed in and out from the town. The homes along the banks of the stream kept small rowboats to cross to the town, making the church and schools and all else very convenient.

This was the beginning of George's opportunities. He grasped these as they came. He had few books at home. Here he had access to literature and to people who were helpful to him. In the summer time when out of school the boys helped on the farm. George would say, "Father, give me a task today so I may finish it early and have time to read." Then he would work with all his might, the perspiration trickling down his face, and far ahead of the others in the rows of corn or vegetables. When the task was completed, he would produce some such book as *Paradise Lost* or a history and stretch himself under the shade of some nearby tree to enjoy his feast. He was not content with once reading, but again and again he would read the same book. He made a mark in the back each time he went through, until there were quite a number of marks. He found an old book somewhere, of English poets. Both backs were off, but that made no difference; he had discovered a gold mine. Here he made the acquaintance of Young's "Night Thoughts," Gray's "Elegy," Byron's "Apostrophe to the Ocean," Milton's "Christmas Hymn," and a host of others, that were his lifelong friends, with which he regaled himself, as well as many of his hearers. The "Christmas Hymn" was invariably read to the family on Christmas morn.

The last time we sat quietly by the broad Pacific, he recited portions of the "Apostrophe to the Ocean." Even when a boy, he never cared for stories, but wanted something to make him think. When a young man his light readings were such as Beecher's *Eyes and Ears* and Talmage's *Crumbs Swept Up,* and other books of that character. Later in life, when his family were about him, he amused the children with Joel Chandler Harris' *Uncle Remus.*

When a half-grown boy he was the one ready in the Sunday school to give the Christmas address or the Fourth of July declamation, and did it with the serious air of a grownup. His stepmother took much pride in his ability and would call him out to read or recite for her on company occasions.

When George was fourteen, his parents deemed it the best thing to permit him to become a student of medicine under Dr. George O. Tyler, who was a fine Christian gentleman, well educated, and a practicing physician in that locality with a pharmacy located in Onancock. He continued his studies there until the breaking out of the Civil War, and for a short time after. But as Virginia had seceded with the rest of the South, the feeling ran high, especially among the young men.

A company was organized which George joined. Later it disbanded, as the Union forces, coming down from the North, were overwhelming; and the two counties of Accomac and Northampton were entirely cut off from the rest of the South by the Chesapeake Bay. Most of the young men ran the blockade across the bay and joined the Southern army over there.

George, with his uncle, George Scarburgh, about his own age, secured passage in one of those boats that made a business of stealing through the darkness to the other side of the bay. It was a perilous journey, as the boat was small and could carry no lights for fear of discovery. The winds were cold, and the boys unprotected. They nearly froze to death. However, a stop at Watts Island for two days relieved the situation somewhat, and they finally landed safely in Urbana on the Rappahannock River. From there they went to Richmond, Virginia, and enlisted in the Forty-sixth Volunteers under Brigadier General Henry A. Wise, also of Accomac County, Virginia. George was in York-town when the town was besieged by General McClelland. After the retreat from there he was in the battle of Seven Pines.

His health became such, from the exposure and hard life, that he did very little active service after this. He became ill and was sent to a hospital for a time. When he returned to his company, he found his two older brothers, John and William, who had crossed the bay and joined his company.

George soon had a relapse and had to return to the hospital on Chapin's farm, and his brother John was sent to nurse him. However, John became ill also; and so the second brother, William, was ordered to nurse both of them. Soon he also became ill. The doctors pronounced George beyond recovery; and, as caskets had to be brought from a distance, his was ordered. Being delirious he knew nothing of what was transpiring. When he recovered consciousness, he was informed that his brother John had passed away. Shortly after, his other brother, William, also was taken. The casket brought for George was used instead for one of his brothers.

When letters reached George from home, his father had also been called suddenly, and on the same day as William had died. Mrs. Watson, his stepmother, said that only a few days before his father's death, the father had come from the secret chamber and told her he had the assurance that George would be converted, and from that time his burden was gone.

A few months afterward there was quite a religious awakening in George's regiment. One night while the meeting was in progress, he, with some other comrades, was playing a game of cards. He was under great conviction for sin. While in the midst of the game, he seemed to hear a voice speaking in his soul, saying, "Now is the time. Unless you give your heart to God now, you will be in torment in a month." This so alarmed him that he threw down the cards, and said, "Boys, this is my last game." He left them and went to the meeting and knelt at the pine log used for an altar. The next night, August 11, 1863, he was blessedly converted.

In September, 1863, his company was sent to Charlestown, South Carolina, under General Beauregard, during the bombardment of that city.

The company spent the winter of 1863 on Johnson's Island, and in the spring of 1864 was ordered to Petersburg, Virginia, where George was again stricken down with illness. This time he was taken to Kittrell Springs, North Carolina, to recuperate. After some improvement in his condition, when he was able to be up, he served in the drug store at that place.

Chapter 3

Enters Life Work

UPON his return home from the army the call to preach the gospel came to him afresh. His health was very seriously impaired because he had been ill so much of the time while away the three years. He could not rest comfortably on a bed after sleeping on the ground so long, and he was reduced to a mere skeleton. It took months, yes, years, to restore him to health. His younger brother, Joseph, with his stepmother and her children, Emma and Richard, made a home for him until he was able to take care of himself. In later years he often referred to his sufferings at that period. The first attempt at any sort of work was a clerkship on Watts Island in the Chesapeake Bay. He there suffered untold agony as the result of his experiences in the army. He has been styled "the child of Providence" by some of his friends, and that surely is appropriate, as we shall see how all through his life, God provided and delivered.

Providentially, he did not have to remain but a few months in that position on the island, but was removed to Onancock to a clerkship with an old friend of his father's, Perry A. Leatherbury, who was also a local Methodist Episcopal preacher and a fine Christian man. His wife was a very motherly woman; and as George was to be a member of the family, she would see that he was well cared for. Here, he was near the church and could attend regularly, which he did, and participated in the services by public prayer and testimony.

At this time a very spiritual young preacher was appointed by the presiding elder, as the supply or assistant preacher to the pastor of Onancock Methodist Episcopal Church, Philadelphia Conference, Rev. Levin P. Causey by name. He had not completed his preparation for the ministry, and at the end of a year's service he decided to go to the Garrett Bible Institute at Concord, New Hampshire, at that time.

He and George saw each other almost daily, and he soon began talking it to George and used his influence in making his decision to accompany his friend and prepare for the ministry. These two were very diverse and yet congenial. If they did not see alike, they agreed to disagree and continued to be friends all the same. They never had an unpleasantness between them, and continued to be loving friends to the day of George's death.

They were both worthy young men; they both were called of God to preach; they both wanted a fitness for it, and they agreed to go together to the same place. This was sufficient to bind them together, and they were both kind and affectionate in disposition. In the autumn of 1865 they arrived at the Institute. George had a very small amount from his father's estate, and he borrowed a little from a friend; and he did not go in debt after that was spent.

In January, 1866, he preached his first sermon, on John 3:18, in a schoolhouse near Concord, New Hampshire. It was a cold, bitter night, such as are had in New England, below zero. Being from the South, he felt it very keenly and says in his notes, "My clothing was insufficient." He did not return there a second year, but went to his home in Onancock, Virginia, where he received the license to preach from Rev. Solomon Cooper, presiding elder of that district. He was sent as supply to the Snow Hill, Maryland Circuit, with Rev. J. H. Kirkpatrick, senior preacher. He made his home with the people, going around from house to house by invitation from those who were so situated as to be able to entertain him. He took his books along, and in this way kept up his conference studies.

At the end of the conference year, in March 1867, he attended his first Conference in Philadelphia, joined on probation and received an appointment as junior preacher to Laurel, Delaware Circuit, with Rev. James Carrol, pastor.

There were ten preaching places. He preached three times each Sunday and rode about thirty miles on horseback. The writer thinks it was at this place that the elder remarked aside to a friend, as he saw the young preacher pass, "Poor fellow, I am afraid he is not long for this world." They had a gracious revival that year in the church just built.

As it was the custom in those days for the junior preacher to remain only one year, he received the appointment the following March, 1868, of junior at Annamessex Circuit, with Rev. T. L. Tomkinson as senior,. who had served the Onancock Church in Virginia, and was also an old friend. This made it very pleasant. The Philadelphia Conference had been divided at this session; and this, the southern part of it, was called Wilmington Conference. During that summer Rev. Tomkinson opened a new appointment on the Annamessex Circuit at Crisfield, Maryland; and George, the junior preacher, delivered the first sermon ever preached there, in an old fishing boat called "Noah's Ark."

In March, 1869, he was promoted to preacher in charge of Newtown, Maryland. On October 7, 1869, he married Miss Margaret Evelyn Watson, of Onancock, Virginia, and they went on a little wedding trip to Washington, D. C. At that time President Grant was in the White House. Dr. J. P. Newman, afterwards Bishop Newman, was pastor of the Metropolitan Methodist Episcopal Church. After a few happy days in the National Capital, the bride and groom took the steamer down the Chesapeake Bay and up the Pocomoke River as far as Newtown, Maryland, afterwards named Pocomoke City, where they received a warm greeting from his church.

This was the first and only year of his pastorate in this place. This charge had always been one of several appointments on a circuit, until this year, when it had been made a station. But it was not able to sustain itself and support a pastor. Hence at the Conference in March, it was put back on the circuit until the town should be sufficiently large to repeat the experiment with success.

The subject of our story was appointed at that time to Frankford, Delaware, with three other country preaching places attached. Those were days when some men did not hesitate to speak their minds and by threats and physical might try to intimidate the preacher of the gospel. George preached a strong temperance sermon at one of the country churches on his charge, on a Sunday. Some hearers disapproved, and the men stood about under the trees in groups, discussing the sermon. Afterwards, one announced his intention of giving the preacher a horsewhipping the next time he came, which would be two weeks from that day. This rude crowd gave it out, and before the next time came it had reached the preacher's ears that the bully would settle with him for his temperance principles. Of course, the curiosity of the people was aroused, and some who would not otherwise have been present were there to see if the preacher would recant and thereby strengthen the intemperate side of the question.

The preacher drove several miles in his buggy to the little country church. He had not armed himself, nor was he in any way prepared for any physical encounter. He remembered the promised horsewhipping for that day, but was in no way disturbed. He had not invited another man to accompany him, and there were no visible signs of his being at all intimidated.

He drove up, alighted, and tied his horse as usual to its accustomed place. He then walked into the church, speaking to the brethren who were standing about the door, and preached his sermon. We do not know the subject, but it in no way weakened the previous one of two weeks ago. His enemy was there; but lo, he had become a friend and gave the preacher a five dollar bill toward a benevolent collection. It was evident that he was ashamed of his former threat and wished, in some way, to atone for it by a gift of money.

CHAPTER 4

Early Pastorate

DURING the summer of 1870, while George was at Frankford, Delaware, the great Oakington National Camp Meeting was held by Rev. Inskip and Alfred Cookman and other members of the Holiness Association. The young pastor was thirsting for such an experience as he knew they taught, having read their writings in accounts of other similar meetings. He also desired greatly to meet those men personally, so when the time came he was there. This meeting was a large one. Hundreds of preachers were present, some coming for a day or two and others for the entire ten days. Thousands of people from many states were in attendance. He heard, for the first time, a sermon on Christian holiness. The preacher who delivered it was Dr. William Butler, returned missionary from India. The text was God's word to Abraham, "Walk before me, and be thou perfect." The second Sunday of the camp meeting the Roman Catholic Church proclaimed in Rome the infallibility of the Pope. This fact was made known by the leader of this meeting, Rev. John S. Inskip, who called the vast audience to stand and sing "All Hail the Power of Jesus' Name." The effect was marvelous and electrifying. At that camp meeting George was led to the altar by Rev. Alfred Cookman to seek the experience of sanctification, but he did not enter fully into the experience. However, he took a stand in faith for the blessing.

On his return to Frankford, he began preaching on the subject and holding special meetings in his home for the promotion of holiness. This was not encouraged by his superior officer, which somewhat cooled his ardor. However, he bore it sweetly and pressed on for the coveted experience. The following poem expresses, in a measure, his glowing enthusiasm under the inspiration of the meeting on that great and last day of the feast at the notorious Oakington Camp Meeting:

A SABBATH AT OAKINGTON, JULY 17, 1870

"Far through the memory shines a happy day."-Lowell

> I drew near to him,
> And he to me, oh, beatific sight!
> Not living only, it endowed new life;
> Not beautiful alone, it beautified;
> Nor only glorious for it glorified."
> —Bickersteth

The human soul is touched with such fine sense
That signalings from God's high realm need not
The loud pronouncing of the world to make
Them heard. God does not call his armies forth
With sounding bugle blasts of boisterous earth;
But by heart yearnings, his best voice in man.
For he who fills and shrouds the all of things
Collides with our most hidden selves, and scans
The woof and color of our life resolve;
If that resolve be furrowed to his will
He'll plant the germ of appetite for God.

Thus by some spirit gravity were drawn
The multitudes in Oakington's fair grove,
For Christ in love devised magnific feasts
In his prime forest temples to be served,
And hunger was the messenger he sent,
To draw the company around his board.
Those banquet days swept by as eagle-winged,
But from their wings, dropped benedictions down;
And in their train was brought the restful day
Which in love's calendar shall ever stand

Like some bright star that rolls and stands apart.
That Sabbath morn walked softly forth from out
The fragrant placid bosom of its God
As Caleb came from the rich Canaan land,
Or rather as a king's chief butler, came
To bear the children wine their Lord had pressed;
And had his golden goblet brimmed so full
That, as he crossed the threshold of the dawn,
He spilled some spicy drops at early prayer.

The hour passed on for royal agape,
And hundreds struck to harmony by love,
Met as the melted snows in valleys meet
By sweet dissolving sympathy convolved,
To pour from sprinkled lips their witness forth,
In that Lamb tryst all hearts and thoughts were free.
The tropic sun of righteousness had thawed
A thousand souls from out the frigid zones
Of sect, and state, and nationalities;
And made them one by love's divine franchise,
There, as they stood upon the hours climax,
With hands and eyes and hearts and voice uplift,
They threw their full devotion into song;
And sent a coronation hymn, fire-fledged,
To him, who heaven rules and earth redeems.

Then heavenly silence reigned, the while each soul
For itself bathed within the cleansing flood.
Words can never syllable that still scene;
While hearts were washed, and minds were purified,
And earth sat dumb beneath the touch of God.
                                        —G. D. Watson

CHAPTER 5

Called West

THE summer soon passed happily, with its toil and its pleasures; and when, in October, the little Luella made her
advent, the Watsons' cup ran over with joy. The young father had
been given to writing poetry for a few years past, and what better
expression could he give of his pleasure than to write the following little verse to the sleeping infant when she was a week old?

> Little babe, why art thou smiling,
>   Wrapt in slumber's downy arms?
> Are some angel bands beguiling
>   Thy young fancy with their charms?
> Are you visiting those regions
>   Down from which you deigned to come,
> And do Heaven's laughing legions
>   Woo you from our earthly home?
>
> Heed them not, sweet dreaming baby,
>   They would steal you from us back;
> Stay on earth, and angels may be
>   Glad to come and guard your track.
> May such smiling fill thy slumber
>   All along thy checkered life,
> And may death, though cold and somber,
>   Leave a smile to deck thy life.

According to the conference order of things, they supposed
now, surely this would be their home for two years; but God was
on the giving hand and he had other things in store. A short while
before Wilmington Conference of 1871 convened, a letter was

received by the young pastor from Mr. James Riddle, the cotton manufacturer of Riddle's Mills on the banks of the Brandywine River near Wilmington, Delaware. A fine old Irish gentleman and local preacher he was, as well as the influential leader in Mt. Salem Methodist Episcopal Church in the suburb of Wilmington. He wished to know if dear Brother Watson would consent to be appointed to his church, if the bishop were willing to make that appointment. He and the church thought they needed such services as he could give them by consenting to be their pastor. His reply was: "I am at the disposal of my superior officer and shall be glad to go to you if he so appoints." That was all.

A few weeks later the pastor sold his carriage and gave his horse to a poor brother who was greatly in need. This was characteristic of his dealings all through life. He was large-hearted and generous almost to a fault. When he had less than a thousand a year, he has invited some poor Christian brother to camp meeting and paid all traveling expenses as well as entertainment.

God never stays in debt to his children long. When the pastor and family reached their new home, they found all in readiness for their comfort: a clean, well-furnished house and the old fashioned cradle with all that belonged to it, just ready for occupancy. The salary was increased by one hundred dollars, besides the perquisite. One tenth of this was the Lord's. The two years' pastorate was fruitful to the church and pleasant to the pastor and family.

Father and Mother Riddle were ever watchful over the occupants of the parsonage to see that all their needs were supplied, including new blankets for Thanksgiving and the check that invariably came each holiday from the stone mansion upon the riverbank.

Their love and sympathy were expressed in many ways when the second little daughter was laid away in the Mt. Salem Cemetery.

In those days George was ever on the alert to learn. Wilmington and nearby Philadelphia furnished Alfred Cookman, Jacob Todd, and others at whose feet he gladly sat and learned of them. He never lost an opportunity of hearing them speak.

His next move was to Dover, Delaware—beautiful Dover, with its comfortable homes, its ornamental shade trees, and its literary, largehearted people.

Being the capital of the state, the congregations were far above the average in intelligence. Ex-Governor Salisbury and his brother, Senator Salisbury, along with Representative Shakespeare, with their families, were members and regular attendants upon the services. Rev. James Williams, principal of the Conference Academy (now Conference Bible Institute), and his wife, were also among the best loved friends of the pastor's family, as were also Dr. Dunning and many others.

The young preacher, in connection with his pastoral duties, served one term as chaplain of the state senate and also Belles-lettres lecturer in the Academy. The church he found in a fine working condition, and the pastorate proved a very happy one for both pastor and people.

While in Dover the pastor and family attended a camp meeting on the old Camden Camp Ground, where Bishop Asbury and Henry Boehm held some wonderful meetings. The latter records that at one camp meeting thirteen hundred were converted and five hundred sanctified. George had the privilege of hearing Father Boehm preach a few years before this, when he was nearly a hundred. His text was, "O Lord, revive thy work," and he spoke thirty minutes in the Asbury Church, Wilmington, Delaware.

During this pastorate, the preacher was invited to attend the reopening of the Methodist Episcopal Church in Princess Anne, Maryland, and to be one of the speakers on the occasion. The other preacher was Dr. Larry Dashiel, the missionary secretary of the Methodist Episcopal Church, from New York. Both of these were native sons of the peninsula, one of Maryland, the other of Virginia. Neither had heard the other preach. This was the beginning of a warm and lasting friendship.

Toward the close of the second year's pastorate, in 1875, Bishop Wylie was looking for a man adapted to take the Meridian Street Methodist Episcopal Church, Indianapolis, Indiana.

Dr. Naylor was leaving in the middle of the conference year for a church in Baltimore. The western conferences meet in autumn, and it was necessary to find an eastern man. The bishop asked Dr. Dashiel if he knew of such a man. He replied, "Yes, George D. Watson, of Dover." He had heard the young man at Princess Anne. This was the link in the chain of Providence. Soon after this George received a letter from Bishop Wylie asking him if he would go to Indianapolis the following spring, when his conference should meet. The humble pastor of Dover was quite overcome when he read the letter and trembled as the strength, beauty, and opulence of this great church were unfolded to him by the writer. Could he, who was just thirty years old, and handicapped as he had been by having no college training, no degree or diploma, attempt to fill such a pulpit? He told the news to his wife, and they together decided it was not a matter to be settled in a moment, nor a day.

While praying and deliberating before settling it, a letter came from the official board of this wonderful church in that far-off western city (as it seemed in those days), requesting him to come out for a Sabbath and meet the people of his prospective audience and let them hear him preach.

Of course a check accompanied the letter, and there seemed no alternative but to go. After the Sabbath closed, they said, "You'll do," and dismissed him with their blessing, to return home and prepare for moving.

CHAPTER 6

Experiences in Indianapolis

DURING these various preceding pastorates many things worthy of note occurred which have not been recorded and have dropped from memory. Suffice it to say, the preacher was always in favor of real revivals of the old-time sort, and each year a special season was devoted to the conversion of souls and the deepening of the spiritual life in the hearts of believers. His sermons, while not always evangelistic, were instructive, very literary, but full of Bible. He often preached on the Holy Spirit; and although he took no active part in holiness work, he felt his need for the experience.

There had been some revival, some real soul-saving and the warming up of the members in each pastorate, and additions to the church. There are always a select few in every place whose lives are hid with Christ in God, who are intercessors for their pastor and the church. The preacher soon finds these; and if he has any soul hunger, he appreciates them and asks their prayers and counsel.

Our preacher always found these saints of God, and they were a great bulwark to him and his work. A letter written shortly after arriving in Indianapolis, to his old friend, Dr. George C. Tyler, under whom he had studied medicine when a boy, gives his impression of his work and surroundings. Here are some extracts:

May 4, 1875:

I had no hand in my appointment here further than to consent to come. This is one of the best charges in the entire Methodist Episcopal Church, and the best in the city. The edifice is of gray stone, and will seat one thousand easily. The membership is about six hundred. My congregation, as a rule, are wealthy, cultivated, and fashionable, but very active and aggressive. Many of my friends feared for me to take such a church; and I could but fear for myself when I remembered my lack of a college education and culture, and then remembered that I was to succeed two college presidents and the eloquent Bishop Bowman (he being elected soon after leaving this pulpit). But God has been very good to me and given me strength so far and favor with this people. They say I am the very man for them, and there is no end to their appreciative words of the sermons. The salary here is more than double that of my former charge, and they are now talking of building a parsonage. In fact, one man has given the first thousand toward that end.

We have fourteen Methodist Episcopal churches in this city, and they are divided between the Indiana and the Southeastern Indiana Conferences. I am in the former. The people are large-hearted and exceedingly kind, sending their carriages around to take us out any time we wish. Yet sometimes we feel a little homesick for the friends we have left behind us.

We took a Pullman Palace car at Philadelphia and came straight through in thirty-three hours and found the journey not very irksome and much of it very interesting, owing to the superb scenery and several great cities.

Many of the preachers in the West did not favor parsonages in those days, as they preferred to buy in the rapidly growing cities and then sell at a profit when they left that pastorate. The new preacher, however, had always been accustomed to the parsonages in the East, and did not favor the Western way. He told his friends he would board the family until the church could build a new home. In his notes he says:

There was a debt of $30,000 on the beautiful new church when I arrived in March, 1875, and I at once resolved to do all I could to pay the debt off. In June of the same year we invited Bishop Thomas Bowman, a former pastor of this church, to spend a Sunday with us, preaching and taking subscriptions for this debt. The effort was so successful that we not only secured the amount needed, but had a balance of $8,000 which was sufficient to build the parsonage.

They immediately broke ground; and in the autumn of 1876, when the preacher's family returned from the East, where they had been spending the summer, they found the new parsonage ready and fully furnished. It was a three-story brick building of eight rooms, besides the third story.

To go back a little in our story, he says in his notes:

> Two months after our arrival, on May 31, 1875, our first son came to gladden our home. We named him Fletcher Guard Watson, and, of course, felt he was to succeed his father in the ministry.
>
> He was also named for Rev. Thomas Guard, whom we had entertained in our home when living in Dover, Delaware, and who was a great orator and a very saintly man as well. At four years of age, Fletcher, when some friend asked the child if he was going to be a preacher like his father, replied, "I don't know whether I shall preach or raise horses or cook."

At a very early age he gave his heart to God, as did the other two children, and he obeyed the call to preach when through school. He entered the Baltimore Conference in 1899, and was transferred to the Southern California Conference in 1915.

Chapter 7

Writing

SHORTLY after entering the ministry, George began to write for the local papers in the little town where he was stationed. His topics were temperance, religion, ethics, and anything helpful. About this time he came in touch with Dr. Adam Wallace, editor of the *Ocean Grove Record,* and engaged to write for him. A few of his old poems and other articles published in that paper have been preserved. Some also were saved from the *Newtown Record,* and others later on from the *Christian Standard* of Philadelphia, the *Christian Witness* of Boston, and the *Christian Advocate* of Michigan, of which Dr. Potts was editor.

While serving Mt. Salem Church, Wilmington, Delaware, he was acting editor for a temperance paper. In 1901 he edited a paper of his own, *Living Words,* a monthly periodical at Pittsburgh. This was discontinued when the family went abroad to New Zealand. He was a regular contributor to the *Way of Faith* during the editorship of Rev. John M. Pike, for a term of about twenty-five years. He also wrote some for *God's Revivalist* of Cincinnati and the *Way of Holiness.*

When he came to Indianapolis he had greatly improved his diction, and his voice was always clear and fluent.

His sermons were never written out in full—only the main points on a few short pages, well studied, and delivered extemporaneously. On entering the pulpit, he took with him a small bit of paper having the main headings on it. It was his custom to prepare his sermons early in the week.

On Sabbath morning he would retire to his study, have a season of prayer, read over his notes, and spend some time reading aloud from such writers as Dr. Hall, Dr. Chalmers, or Faber.

He received many letters from preachers asking how to succeed. All of these he urged to "take time to prepare." He had no patience with the man who left off, until Saturday, the preparation of a sermon.

After he came to Indianapolis, his sermons appeared very often on Mondays in the local press. These have never been given in book form, but a few are preserved in an old scrapbook. Among these we find the following sermons: "The Church's Guardianship Over the World," "Am I My Brother's Keeper?" "Thanksgiving," "The Slavery of Work," "Pentecost," and "The Sovereignty of the Heart." These give some idea of his study and work at this time. One of the aged preachers of the conference asked his daughter, who attended Dr. Watson's church, "What does your preacher talk about most?" She replied, "He speaks a great deal about the Holy Spirit." "That is fine," the old saint replied. The following will serve to illustrate, and is taken from his sermon on "Pentecost."

> Text—Acts 2:1: "And when the day of Pentecost was fully come." The day of Pentecost was not an isolated event. It had its roots in the past. There is no event or text in the Bible that stands out solitary and alone. In the Bible the great days and events correspond, and echo to each other across intervening distances of space and time. This is an evidence that the Book was fashioned under an intelligence that was superior to nature and time. As a master shipbuilder selects his materials from many forests, so the architect of the Bible has gathered from the forests of history characters and events that fit into one another to construct the ark of truth. The word Pentecost signifies the fiftieth day and was first instituted at the giving of the law. We find many parallelisms between the giving of the law and the descent of the Holy Spirit. The law was given at the beginning of the Hebrew church and priestly administration. The Holy Spirit was given at the beginning of the Christian church and apostolic administration. Across the valley of fifteen centuries Mt. Sinai and Mt. Zion answered each other.
>
> 1) By placing the first and last Pentecosts together we get a twofold revelation of divine government.

While all things are under God's government, all things are not controlled by the same species of authority. One is the authority of law, the other is the authority of love. At the first Pentecost, at Sinai, the Deity unfolded to mankind the dominion of law with all its inflexible and coercive principles and penalties—a law that took hold of man merely as creatures of government, a law that was external to man's tastes and affections, and hence was appropriately inscribed on tablets of stone. At the last Pentecost on Mt. Zion there was established a spiritual dominion within man, with an authority written upon the tablets of the heart, which swayed men by the constraining forces of affections.

The authority of the first Pentecost told men what they ought to do. The authority of the last Pentecost told men what they could do. Mt. Sinai's law was like a mighty vise, seizing in its iron grasp the hard hearts of men to press them into the divine image. But Jerusalem's baptism was a heated furnace that melted the leaden affections of men and poured them into the mold of Christ. God controls nature, fallen spirits, and the motives of men by the empire of unyielding law; and that empire reached its culmination at Sinai. God controls his holy angels, the spirits of the just, and his children by the empire of love, and that empire reached its culmination at the last Pentecost. All moral beings are under one or the other of these dominions.

2) By placing the first and last Pentecosts together, we gather a twofold revelation of God's communion with man. If there is any period at which it is eminently fitting for the Deity to let himself down into communion with man, it is when he comes forth from the shroud of eternity to institute a great moral dispensation. Hence, at the beginning of the Hebrew and Christian dispensations, we behold God offering himself to the fellowship of man. But look at the difference between these two occasions. You have read how the Divinity stationed his glory on the mountain top, how the people were assembled around its base with no intervening barrier between them, and how he sought to pour directly into their hearing the plenitude of wisdom and law. Though there were no external bars between them, yet there was a mighty internal and spiritual

barrier in man's nature which hindered the free communion of God. At the last Pentecost, where the same Deity descended in a chariot of thunder upon the Christian church on Mt. Zion, mark the plenary communion of God on that occasion. The internal barrier had been cut away by the rushing tide of the Savior's blood. Man's nature had been deepened into wondrous capacity, and without hindrance Deity flows freely into man.

3) The union of these two great days presents us a twofold revelation of divine speech.

Speech is the noblest medium between God and man. It is the highest instrument creature mind can wield, and the highest instrument that God knows.

As Christ renders God intelligible to man, he is denominated "The Word." But there have been two great eras of divine speech in the world, the one supernatural and the other incarnate.

The first period began in Eden, when the voice of the Lord floated in the twilight and brought consternation to the guilty man. This era reached its climax at Mt. Sinai, when the sound of a trumpet and the voice of words, as if articulated from the lurid lips of clouds, terrified the whole nation.

The next great era of divine speech began with the preaching of Jesus, the incarnate Word, and reached its climax in the last Pentecost, when the emblem of the fiery tongues sat on the brows of the disciples. The tongues were like fire, denoting the cleansing and enlightening power of divine words. They sat on the brow, which is the center of intelligence and will. They were cleft into many branches, denoting that God's truth was to run out through all the languages of the earth. The same divine speech which terrified the Hebrew church became to the Christian church a source of ecstasy and weapon of power.

The first era of speech was external to man, spoken from lips of air and cloud.

The second era became incarnate in man, and was spoken from the depth of the soul. The era of external speech serves to condemn the world. The era of internal speech wins and redeems the world.

At the last Pentecost the babbling dialects of the earth,

like separate chords in one harp, had been tuned to such accord that the auditorium of nature was filled with an irresistible symphony. As long as the Word of God is kept out of the heart we are under Mt. Sinai. If we receive it into our hearts we are under the last Pentecost.

CHAPTER 8

Seeks Perfect Love

MANY things conspired during this pastorate to reveal the high estimation in which the pastor was held in the hearts of his people. The congregations were large and very appreciative, and no opportunity was lost to them to do him honor. His pulpit was to him the grandest place on earth. He was in great demand as well in educational circles. Invited to preach at the Asbury College (afterwards the DePauw University) at Greencastle, Indiana, his sermon so impressed his audiences that the degree of Doctor of Divinity was given to him. Later he addressed the literary societies of the State University in Bloomington, Indiana. Of this the press remarks:

> To say it was good is not enough. It was a surprise, though Dr. Watson was favorably known by reputation, yet many of our people had no idea of his great abilities. That he is a man of great abilities was evidenced by his effort here last evening. His subject was "America's Future Literature," a subject, it will be at once seen, which involves the discussion of abstractions, yet in the hands of this brilliant orator glowed like an epic. Dr. Watson is a coming man, mark this prediction. The annual addresses in the past have been delivered by distinguished personages, but this is the first one which has ever been delivered extemporaneously.

Following this he was honored with election to the Phi Kappa Psi fraternity. These honors were very gratifying to him, but did not satisfy the deeper longings of his heart. His own words are:

> I had hours of sweet communion with God, but they were unsteady; and I had a great deal of soul twilight. I loved to

51

preach and enjoyed a revival, felt much enthusiasm in all the interests of my church, felt at home only in Christian society, and was thrilled with the grandeur and harmony of Bible truth. I felt my whole life to be one unending *will struggle.* I somehow felt that my volition was kept in a strain as if pushing itself through the piled-up duties of each day.

My years were filled with crumbled resolutions to be more courageous, industrious, Christlike, etc., just as if Christlikeness came by will power. I felt anxious about my work and my success. The very word *work* became a complete world to me. I was ambitious to keep my pulpit up to the highest pitch possible. Every night I counted the unfinished tasks, and numbered the persons I wanted to visit, and could not for lack of time. For years my motto was *hard work* with double emphasis on the *hard.*

I felt that disappointment, trouble, sickness in my family was often rather hard to endure. When the burden was heavy, I would weep and feel rebellious alternately. I was often impatient toward men, especially professed Christians. I, too, often allowed myself to become vexed at the inconsistencies of my church members. I lived every day knowing that my heart, will, and life were not up to the Bible standard and that there were whole chapters and many verses of Scripture which I did not experience. Even when I regarded holiness as only a growth in grace, I *knew* that those who professed perfect love had an experience that I had not. I suffered more than tongue can tell from melancholy. An unkind or unfavorable criticism, or an apparent neglect, would often hurl my spirits into the deepest gloom. As the result of all these elements in my life, I grew *tired.* My soul and body seemed to ache through and through with weariness. I grew tired of living in the public eye, tired of routine work, but most of all tired of myself. I found my mind lingering upon the calmness of Christ's life, the fact that Christ was never hurried, never overcrowded, and never excited, until I longed to have his freedom from anxiety and his heart rest.

Being separated so far from earlier friends, I felt my heart blindly reaching out to clutch some all-explaining, all-satisfying friend. My soul was drawn out very much in prayer. There were seasons in which I never grew weary in praying. For many weeks I felt the spirit of supplication growing more intense, taking at times the form of conversation with Christ. I grew very teachable. I quit my mental habit of philosophizing about every phenomenon. I knew that I was very ignorant and very little. I was willing to be taught by anybody, and every day for a week, any deeper spiritual truth.

I saw as plain as day that many things that I and the church at large called infirmities, in God's sight were sinful and ugly. I saw as I had never seen that "whatsoever was not of faith was sin." December 1, 1876, in the parsonage of the Meridian Street Church, Indianapolis, at midnight, after an hour of prayer, I felt a willingness to turn my body, soul, and spirit over to the will of Christ, absolutely and eternally, without any reservation. Instantly many suggestions were presented to my mind, some of them absurd, but I answered them all positively and immediately. I had never felt that my cigar was a sin, but that night when Jesus whispered, "Will you abandon your tobacco that your body may be my clean temple?" I answered at once, "Yes, Lord." Then Jesus whispered, "Will you go anywhere on earth that I may send you? Will you suffer willingly and without a murmur, anything that I may send in your life? Are you willing to be just as holy and spotless as I want you? Knowing that the experience of entire sanctification is so little understood and so much opposed by many preachers and church members, will you in the face of all this stand before the ministry, the church and the world, and confess me before men as your complete Sanctifier? Will you never preach a sermon or undertake anything without seeking especially to please me? Will you freely consent to die at any time, in any place and in any manner that will glorify me?" To all these inner whisperings, I answered with a melted heart, "Yes, precious Jesus, I am entirely yours. Do as you please with me and through me, now and forever." I then fell asleep.

Next morning, Saturday, December 2, I awoke finding my appetite for tobacco nearly all gone and my mind set against it. I also felt very calm and peaceful, but did not regard it as the result for which I was seeking. The only remaining step was faith.

That day a meeting for Christian holiness was held in my church (the Meridian Street Methodist Episcopal Church). That afternoon in that meeting I repeated in my heart the limitless consecration of the night previous, and at the same time I determined to claim, accept, and confess Christ as my Sanctifier and limitless Savior, then and there. I knew that my consecration was entire, and so I found faith was easier than I had ever known before. I was not seeking a baptism of joy. I was tired of myself and was simply seeking to get myself consciously out of my own hands over entirely into the hands of Christ. I had but little concern what God would do in me or for me. I simply determined that my consecration and faith should be entire and then let the matter rest.

When I sank down in an act of heart trust on Christ's complete saving power, everything within me became as quiet and still as the grave. There were points in my consecration like nails of crucifixion, but now that the death-line had been crossed, I felt quiet and serene as if sleeping with Jesus in his pulseless tomb. I never felt so rested in my life. The rest of my soul was imparted to my body. "His rest shall be glorious" became a reality. The long battle of will, all anxiety, all personal ambition, all fret, worry, and care were annihilated. All my care was literally cast on the Lord.

I remained in this state of mind from Saturday to Monday afternoon. I had spent a season in prayer, reading chapter one of 1 Peter, when the Holy Spirit applied the eighth to my heart with unutterable power and glory. The spiritual resurrection power spoken of by Paul in Colossians 3 and Romans 6 was a matter of consciousness. My conversion was powerful and sweet, but this was positively "unspeakable and full of glory." I had a distinct consciousness that Jesus made my heart pure. Out of that heart purity I had intuitions, perceptions, and imaginations of God that were wonderful and blissful beyond all words. "Blessed are the pure in heart: for they shall see God," was fulfilled in my heart. I was not aware of anything in my soul but love. I *knew* that all prejudice, all spirit of criticism, all intellectual pride, all impatience, and everything like self-seeking were washed away, and I was full of love. The Bible was wonderful and powerful. I found the life of holiness all through it, found that God gave us present-tense promises, and the words of inspiration entered my mind with a luminous flash. Christ's indwelling was a matter of positive faith and much assurance. There is nothing in my experience that is not found in the Word of God. The 35th chapter of Isaiah and the 13th of 1 Corinthians have become my experience. And I know that my precious Savior, by the Holy Spirit, has done this work in me.

The meeting he refers to was a three days' meeting, planned by the little band in the church who held a weekly meeting for the promotion of holiness.

Mr. Mason was the leader. Mrs. Lucy Stagg was one of the prominent members of the band, along with Mrs. Israel Taylor (wife of the treasurer),and Mr. Carr, with many others of the same faith and experience.

These, with the consent of the pastor and the official board, had invited some speaker of Cincinnati (I think Dr. and Mrs. Pearne), to come and conduct this three days' meeting.

From this time his style of ministry underwent a great change.

CHAPTER 9

The Bondage of Love

O! sweet will of God, thou hast girded me round
    Like the deep moving currents that girdle the sea;
With omnipotent love is my poor nature bound,
    And this bondage to love sets me perfectly free.

For years my will wrestled with vague discontent,
    That like a sad angel o'ershadowed my way,
And the light of my soul oft with darkness was blent,
    And my heart ever longed for an unclouded day.

My wild will was captured, yet under the yoke,
    There was pain and not peace at the press of the load,
Till the glorious burden the last fiber broke,
    And I melted like wax in the furnace of God.

And now I have flung myself recklessly out,
    Like a chip on the stream of the infinite will,
And I pass the rough rocks with a smile and a shout,
    And I just let my God his great purpose fulfill.

I care not for self; all my blisses and pains,
    I gladly yield up to the mandate above,
My crosses and triumphs, my losses and gains;
    I bury them all in the vortex of love.

And now my King Jesus has all his own way,
    I wait but to catch his low whispering word;
'Tis my bliss to behold his gold scepter's bright sway,
    And my triumph I see in each step of my Lord.

Roll on, checkered seasons, bring smiles, or bring tears,
  My craft calmly floats on the infinite tide.
I shall soon touch the shore of eternity's years,
  And near the white throne of my Savior abide.
                                        —G. D. Watson

In his notes, Dr. Watson says, "When I received the baptism of the Holy Spirit on December 14, 1876, it revolutionized everything in my experience and in my thinking and preaching." The Bible became an open book to him. Its pages were flooded with the light of the Spirit. He found sermons everywhere and he never tired of the beauty and depth of much that he had not before understood. He studied the Word with a relish he never had before known, and his Bible readings scintillated with a vital truth that took hold on people. His enthusiasm enthused others. His desires for revivals were intensified, and he at once began planning for special meetings to that end.

Mrs. Jennie Fowler Willing, wife of Dr. Willing, of Illinois, and the sister of Bishop Fowler, was just entering the field of evangelism, and was one of the first women to do so. She was deeply spiritual, working on holiness lines and conversion of souls. She was a very cultured lady and well fitted in every way, easily adapting herself to different people and methods, without compromise. This was the worker chosen by the pastor and church of Meridian Street to lead its hosts on to victory.

Before coming to Meridian Street Church, Indianapolis, Mrs. Willing had been conducting services in Greencastle, Indiana. There had been a fine revival and much had been accomplished among the young people of the university. One young woman who was very promising in her work among the younger people of Greencastle accompanied Mrs. Willing to Indianapolis to assist her here in the work. This was the beginning of the career of another successful worker.

The time for a revival was ripe in Meridian Street Church, and the Lord poured out his Spirit in a wonderful way. It began with large audiences in the main auditorium; but soon it overflowed and two meetings were held at the same time, one in the auditorium above, by Mrs. Willing, and the other in the Sunday school room below, by the pastor.

The meeting progressed with great power for several weeks. About two hundred people converted, and eighty who sought and found the experience of a clean heart were the results of this meeting. It was the first revival of this kind ever in the church. The entire church received a quickening. The prayer meetings were enlarged and enlivened and the class meetings were overflowed.

The next appointment was Trinity Methodist Episcopal Church, Evansville, Indiana. This was a large church, the next in the conference. Here was also a great revival and large congregations. Three pastors in succession had removed after one year, among these being Rev. Earl Cranston, afterwards bishop.

At the time of Dr. Watson's coming to the Trinity Church in Evansville, the Baptist church was without a regular pastor, and many of its members attended the Methodist church, being drawn there by the new preacher and their hunger for spiritual food.

This was in 1877. The pastor invited Dr. William McDonald, editor of *The Holiness Advocate,* and Rev. J. A. Wood, author of *Perfect Love,* both men prominent members of the National Holiness Association, to come for a ten days' meeting to Trinity Church. They stopped at the parsonage during the time. It was a great treat to the people at large; but some, of course, were strongly opposed to the teaching of a second work of grace. However, God blessed his truth as it was preached. Very many souls declared they had never seen it on this fashion, and they were truly lifted to a higher plane of experience; and many others were graciously converted.

At the end of the conference year, Dr. Watson accepted an invitation to go to Centenary Church, New Albany, Indiana, the home of Mr. W. C. DePauw, who was a member of Centenary Church. He, Mr. DePauw, had obtained the experience of holiness some years previous to this. Each week since he had known the experience he had held a meeting in this church for the promotion of heart purity. He was known throughout the country for the stand he had taken and for being a prominent businessman of great wealth as well. The pastor and his family were received into his hospitable home and heartily welcomed by Mr. and Mrs. DePauw for the first week and until the parsonage was ready for their occupancy. Such a Christian spirit is rarely found in homes of today. There was always time for the family altar, always time for manifestations of kindness to each other, and broad hospitality toward the friend and visitor. This was the man who endowed the old Asbury College with one million dollars, and it was so much appreciated that the college took the new name of DePauw and became a university. In the Centenary Church at New Albany, the pastorate was both pleasant and profitable. Some good revival services were held, and the church was left in fine working condition at the end of this pastorate.

During this pastorate at Centenary Methodist Episcopal Church, Dr. Watson was threatened with a nervous breakdown, and his congregation gave him a month's rest and sent him to Florida. There at Arlington he met a number of old friends from Ocean Grove. He says:

> Here with these friends amid blooming orange trees, groves of moss-covered live oaks and sighing pines, with mocking birds, squirrels, and an ideal temperature, I had the most restful week that I have had for many years. I was delighted with my four weeks' sojourn in Florida, was much benefited in bodily health, and must confess to a little falling in love with the climate. I returned home in time to meet a March snowstorm!

There are always sad recollections with the pleasant ones, like the thorn among the lovely roses. Little George Edward, who had come into their home two years before, sickened and left them in a few hours, during the intense heat of the last summer of their stay in New Albany. Though so young, he could sing, in his baby language, "Around the Throne of God in Heaven," keeping the tune very nicely.

At the annual conference held in the New Albany church, in the autumn of 1880, a delegation was there from Grace Church, Newport, Kentucky, requesting the transfer of Dr. Watson to the Kentucky conference, that he might become its pastor. This was favorable to all concerned; hence in a few weeks he, with his little family of wife, one daughter, and one son, were pleasantly and happily located in the city of Newport, on the Ohio River, just across from Cincinnati. Dr. A. B. Leonard, the father of Bishop Leonard, was at that time pastor of Walnut Hills (Cincinnati) Methodist Episcopal Church. Afterward he became the missionary secretary. Dr. Watson found in Grace Church a worthy people and a fine working force who readily and zealously followed their leader whithersoever he led under the blessing of the Lord.

The church building was renovated—the walls, the pews, and the floors. A revival began which continued for three years. Not less than ten young men and young women decided on Christian work, and some became well known for their services. Many were the conversions and additions.

Dr. Watson was being invited to neighboring churches to conduct revivals, and to Ocean Grove and other camp meetings in the East, in the summer time, and was feeling that God was calling him to give his entire time to that work. By the time his three years were up, he had become settled in the conviction that he must give his entire time to evangelism. He worked so incessantly the last year, keeping up his own work, and outside work besides, that another nervous breakdown came on. This time he accompanied Dr. A. B. Leonard and Mr. William Scarlett, one of his own official members, to Florida for a season. He was regarded the invalid, for the nervous attack was more intense than the previous one had been.

He tells something of his trip in a letter to the papers, to the *Philadelphia Standard.*

Perhaps never a happier visit was made to Florida than that made by the party of three full salvation Methodists who left

Cincinnati in a snowstorm on February 28. Rev. A. B. Leonard, D. D., the brave, strong holiness presiding elder of East Cincinnati district; Mr. W. W. Scarlett, of Dunn's Mercantile Agency and a generous, anointed class leader; and my little half-broken-down self, composed the party. How our hearts have been woven into deeper, never-to-be-forgotten love! What inimitable freedom and transparency has there been between us! Put together the singing on the cars and steamboats and in country boardinghouses, the little prayer meetings in our private room, the full salvation testimony in country meetings and negro cabins, the moonlight stroll through moss-draped forests, the long journeys in mule carts (snail express), the rambling through orange groves, the native peals of innocent wildwoods laughter, the sailing on river and bay, and pacing together the pebbly shore of the ocean. Then add to this a perfect climate, where you suffer from neither heat nor cold, and you have a faint picture of our three weeks in Florida.

I, being the invalid of the party, always received the lion's share of sympathy and attention. Truly the goodness of God swells upon us with an ever increasing wave as we near the golden shore. It has been suggested that a holiness camp meeting be held in the neighborhood of DeLand next February. May the Lord open the way for it.

It is now ten o'clock at night, and from the fourth story of the Florida House in St. Augustine I can see the blazing torch of the lighthouse across the little bay, and beyond that, league on league of old Atlantic, the roar of whose billows is wafted to me through my open window, where I pen these lines and say goodnight. St. Augustine, Florida, March 17, 1881.

He also tells of old Uncle Jack, who was brought from Africa at the age of seven, at this time living in a hut all alone. When they offered to sing for him, he wept and said, "T' ank God. He is so good. He send kind white friends to sing for poor ole Jack."

When this party returned home, they were all greatly benefited, and Dr. Watson entered upon his work with new zeal, but more than ever determined to take up the evangelistic work.

Although he had several solicitations from other very desirable appointments, he asked for the appointment of evangelist and received it at the next conference. He was suffering from swollen hands from rheumatism, and the young daughter had catarrh which prevented her from hearing perfectly during the winter season, and also from attending school regularly. Hence it was decided best to seek a milder climate for the winter, and Florida was chosen at that time as the best.

> I love the virgin's precious Babe,
>> I love his darling cries and tears,
> I love him in his Egypt's flight,
>> And all through his sweet infant years.
>
> I love him at twelve years of age,
>> When his young feet the Temple trod,
> Outwitting doctor, priest, and sage,
>> With his bright wisdom fresh from God.
>
> I love him in his mother's home,
>> Through all those wondrous hidden days,
> With Godhead splendors folded up
>> 'Neath irksome toil and patient ways.
>
> I love him at the Jordan stream,
>> When Heaven opened o'er his brow,
> And the third Person on him came,
>> Like to a dove as white as snow.
>
> I love him through his years of toil,
>> As he poured forth a ceaseless tide
> Of self-surrender, truth, and love,
>> To win my spirit to his side.
>
> I love him all the bleeding way,
>> From Pilate's hall to cruel cross,
> From his sweet death I drink his life,
>> And all my gain is from his loss.

I love him rising from the tomb;
  Like Magdalene, would clasp him there;
And as he to the Father soars,
  My heart floats with him through the air.

I love him dwelling in my breast,
  And by his Spirit spreading through
My soul, his presence, calm and sweet,
  As on parched flowers the healing dew.

I love him coming in the clouds,
  To gather up his gentle Bride,
And banquet with him in the air,
  Where all love's prayers are satisfied.
                    —G. D. Watson

CHAPTER 10

Enters Evangelistic Field

DURING the pastorate of three years in Grace Episcopal Church, Newport, Kentucky, a continuous revival had progressed. The meeting advertised itself by the genuineness of the work. Among many interesting occurrences, we will relate one.

In a barbershop located in the city, the proprietor of which was a leader among his companions, a number of men had collected for professional services. The proprietor suggested that they all go to the meeting that night at Grace Church for, he said, "I have heard that the preacher is a regular fool."

At the proper hour they were there in the meeting. The barber had never heard such truth, since he was no churchgoer. The two-edged sword cut right and left, and the arrows of truth pierced his heart. As soon as the opportunity was given, he was at the altar seeking God. His conviction was powerful and the change wrought in him was marvelous.

He was an ignorant man in all that pertained to salvation or godly terms; and when he felt the change wrought in him, he was in a new world and had no words to express his feelings. He tried very hard to do so, and everyone knew what had happened; but his words were such as he used in street parlance, slang expressions. He sought the blessing of cleansing and baptism of the Holy Ghost the same week, and there was a wonderful illumination given him. He became refined and intelligent, and the call for service came to him. Shortly after a friend assisted him in securing some education and he went out finally with Dr. Godbey, we think it was, in evangelistic work.

A large number of that congregation were called to some kind of public Christian service. Such interest was manifest in

the subject of sanctification that one of the brethren suggested that Dr. Watson prepare a small book of Scripture verses on
that subject with a few apt words on each and publish it, so that
each could have one in his pocket and be prepared for answering
questions that were being asked him concerning the scriptural-
ness of the doctrine. This was his first book, *The Holiness Manual*.
It was afterwards combined with *Steps to the Throne* and has taken
that name.

Grace Church was his last pastorate. The conference was
held in early autumn of about 1880, when he was appointed
evangelist. Some weeks were filled with dates of meetings before
going south to Florida. One meeting was in Kentucky with Dr.
Godbey and Brother Jarrell and others. Another meeting was in
Philadelphia with Dr. Levy in the Baptist Church. Before entering the work, he determined to accept calls from any evangelical
denomination and that all offerings were to be voluntary. It is a
testing experience to anyone to leave a home and a living, provided by the people, and step out by faith—more especially if
there are small children to be cared for. There were three, and the
smallest less than three years old.

God is always on time and his hand was underneath all
the demands of this family as it is of all others who trust him
and claim his promises. There were times of more abundance,
and others which called for greater economy. Of course, he
was watching for all God's pointers, and each strengthened his
convictions. One day in Dr. Levy's home he observed a motto,
"Endure hardness, do the work of an evangelist." This confirmed
him as it came just at that time when he needed all the faith he
could summon. He was never known to utter a word like a regret
that he took that step.

Shortly after Dr. Watson's decision to evangelize, and his
appointment to this work, the first great holiness meeting was
held in Augusta, Georgia. Rev. John S. Inskip and Rev. William
McDonald were the leaders of this meeting. The breach between
the northern body of the Methodist Episcopal Church and the
Church South had been very wide, since the Civil War especially,

and nothing could ever bring them to a friendly feeling except God's intervention.

A torch, however, had been carried through the Holiness Association in the North, of which Rev. Inskip was president, and his desire was to follow it up with a great union meeting, if there could be an opening. The South was ripe to the harvest, and this was the beginning.

One of the pastors of the Methodist Episcopal Church South, with approval of the others, opened his doors to the president of the Association, for a union holiness convention. Mr. Inskip accepted and brought with him as many as possible to assist in the meeting, and also many visitors. Augusta opened its arms and most beautifully welcomed and entertained in homes and hotels all who came. The spirit was most cordial. God in turn opened the windows of Heaven and sent showers of blessings. No mind can ever compute the prejudices broken down and the victories won for Christ's kingdom in those ten days of blessing. It was surely like days of Heaven on earth to workers and people.

The preachers and people poured in from all the cities and country around to attend that meeting. As the fire fell, they wept and rejoiced together and were made hungry for such scenes and experiences in their home churches. They were not willing to see those workers all return North without more of these meetings.

The pastor from Anderson, South Carolina, was in attendance at Augusta, and he engaged Dr. Watson to come to Anderson and give them a ten day's meeting as early as possible. It was arranged for at once as Dr. Watson was already so near by.

Among the home workers in the South, the writer recalls Dr. Godbey, Rev. Jarrell, Rev. Dodge, and also Brother Oliver and his wife, the latter having founded *The Way of Faith*. The last two accompanied Dr. Watson and wife, and Mrs. Bangs of Philadelphia, to Anderson for the prospective meeting. At that time Anderson had a few thousand population. It was not yet recovered from the cruel effects of the war. This Methodist Church had been built some time before the war and was sadly in need of everything. The pastor had been to Augusta and was aflame for God, and he was right to lose no time in bringing about a change at his own church.

When the evangelist and visitors reached Anderson, everyone there was tense with suspense. They had come to a place in their history when something had to be done or the church would expire. As a last resort they had consented to invite this evangelist of the North to come for the meeting as the pastor had requested it, but they appeared awfully frightened lest something might occur which should be out of the regular order. However, all were courteous but very cautious.

A young lawyer, who was a YMCA worker and also a member of the state legislature, came to the station to meet the evangelist and conduct him to the hotel. The people felt afraid yet to invite him to their homes. On Sunday morning they came, filling the church, and listened attentively and eagerly without prejudice. Many hungry souls began to say to themselves, but not to anyone else, "That is the kind of religion I want." In the afternoon a testimony meeting was held, but few had anything to relate except the visitors. At the evening meeting the Lord began to work among the people, and they all seemed to move with one impulse. The young lawyer was kneeling at the altar dying out, as we could see from his expression. The probate judge was on bended knees giving up; and many, many others were also.

This was only the beginning. The evangelist had attended many Nationals, but none had been quite like this. He witnessed such scenes as were never before nor since, in so short a time. The pastor was called to the mission field and went in a few months. The probate judge received the baptism of the Holy Ghost and was called to preach, and afterward edited *The Way of Faith*. The young lawyer renounced his law and legislature and entered the ministry and later became a holiness evangelist. Several others were called to public service, and the church as a whole were ready with songs and testimonies as never before. A boys' private school became so interested that school work was suspended for the time being, in order to permit the boys to attend the services.

Shortly after a new church was built. Calls for work came in from every direction, and for some years the evangelist and family

spent winters in the South—Georgia, the Carolinas, and Florida—and summers farther north. One call came from Mobile, for
a ten day's meeting with the Methodist Church South. Dr. Watson had gone to Florida for the winter and planned to go from
DeLand up the St. John's River as far as Jacksonville; and there
he and his wife and little son traveled by rail west to Mobile,
Alabama. The train was the most antiquated they had ever seen.
There were no upper berths, and the lights were candles in holes
made for that purpose in the arm of each seat. The conductor
said that was its last trip. When they reached Mobile, they were
met at the station by an official member of the church, Judge
Price Williams, who entertained them in his palatial home right
royally. A suite of rooms were theirs to occupy.

When the evening dinner was to be served, and they appeared
in the dining room where the judge introduced them to each
member of his family, lifting his hand he said, "Now before we
take our seats, I want to sing the 'Doxology' in praise to God
for permitting me to live to see this hour when I can have these
friends in my home. This man I have read of and so much desired
to see him." After the Doxology, we were seated at the table on
which was a most sumptuous feast. This dear saint of God had
been reading for many years *The Christian Standard*, edited by Dr.
Pepper, and knew by name many of the Christian workers. He
had not had the privilege of attending the spiritual feasts that are
spread in many parts of the country annually. It was he who had
suggested to the pastor to hold this meeting. He enjoyed it to
the fullest extent, and some others entered into Canaan; but not
much of a revival was had there. They were glad to have the meeting; but Mobile was not ripe, and the pastor was not in perfect
accord, although he did not oppose the doctrine of perfect love.
This was Brother Williams' meeting. I have no doubt God has
given it to him in answer to his prayers. The others only assented
to have it, but he was heart hungry.

Another glimpse we must not neglect to have is the work
among the poorer classes in the cotton mills. Of course, there
were no laws prohibiting child labor and compelling education

at that time, and the people were glad to have something in their midst, of benefit financially, that a child could do. Sometimes the mothers also engaged in weaving. One child, not more than half grown, managed more looms than one. If the threads broke, the loom stopped automatically and the child could readily see where the break was; and she had been taught how to mend it. Housing was better in some places than others, but most of it was very poor. However, it was better than these people could provide for themselves, and they were glad to have it at all. In one place we were told that the evangelist had been invited to the one house with glass lights in it, except that of the manager. Some friends went to assist in the meeting. They had board windows, which kept out rain and snow; but it also kept out the light.

The seeds were sown in these hearts and some fruit was brought forth; but, as usual, conditions hindered the full work. The South, at that time, had advanced much since the war; but much more needed doing. Some of the old log houses of other days were at that time considered tenantable. Suppose the lean-to did not have a glass window—the door could be opened to admit the light of day, by which the evangelist proved the ability to adjust his collar and brush his hair, as well as in a palace.

When surroundings were like this, a very little money was highly valued, and the preacher knew these people could not make one very rich; but he recalled a sentence like this: "The trial of faith is more precious than gold," and so the preacher poured out the hot truth and gave them the best he had to give with much prayer and tears.

Over and over, yes deeper and deeper,
My heart has been pierced with life's sorrowing cry;
But the tears of the sower and the songs of the reaper
Shall mingle together in joy by and by.

CHAPTER 11

Various Meetings

IT is very interesting to note God's way of distributing opportunities to those who have lived in out-of-the-way places, and seemingly in neglected portions of the world.

When that locality in Florida was chosen by Dr. Watson for a winter home, no one could then see the outcome.

It was five miles from everywhere. The railway station, any town at all, or conveniences of any sort, were reached by the slowest method except walking. The roads were sandy and heavy, and horses were slow.

The country road was the main attraction as it led to other towns both ways. The immense live oaks that lined the road on either side were heavily draped with Spanish moss, which swayed lazily in the Florida breeze, and spoke rest and time for everything to tired and nervous men and women from the North and elsewhere.

The soil in this locality had been cleared and tilled for many years. Thus it was ready for building purposes.

Lake Newman, about eight miles long and five miles wide, abounding in fish and alligators, was another charm to the syndicate, for locating there.

People from various states, in quest of health, went there for the winters; and many located permanently.

A church was built, and it became a center of religious activity in the locality.

It was there that conventions for the spreading of scriptural holiness were held with such men as Drs. Reddy of New York and Cullis of Boston, and others from North and South.

The people came in from everywhere around and filled the church to overflowing.

These were red-letter days for that community. Eternity alone will reveal whether they embraced it or not, but there will surely be some to testify to having received the light of full salvation at that time. That was their opportunity. After the Great Freeze of 1894, all left who could get away, and the town was dead.

Another interesting glimpse has filled our mind all these years, since our eyes beheld the wonderful landscapes, and we felt the heart throbs of those excellent Canadian people, with whom we mingled at Toronto.

For several years in succession, Dr. Watson was engaged to participate in those conventions held annually in that city by the Christian workers. The largest hall in Toronto was secured, and the best workers possible. Three times each day for ten days the hall was well filled, and during the day different subjects pertaining to salvation and missions were dealt with.

Testimonials also had a large place in these meetings. It was here that we first met that wonderful woman, Holy Ann, as she was called. Many did not know her last name because she was known by this all over the country. Her main business was to tell of the things God had done for her, and to glorify his name. She always had Scripture verses appropriate to hand out, whether she knew the people or not; and it was remarkable how they fitted.

The evenings were devoted to evangelistic services. A red-hot sermon, and the altar was open for the penitents, or those who were desirous of the fullness of the blessing of the gospel of peace.

During the early part of his evangelistic years, Dr. Watson went regularly to the camp meetings held at Clear Lake, Iowa. He has a report of one of which he had written:

> What a volume of celestial sweetmeats could be compiled, if some invisible or ubiquitous stenographer would report verbatim the sermons, prayers, testimonies, exhortations, and holy conversations of a camp meeting. Here I am on the grass,

under the shade, this summer afternoon, two weeks after the Clear Lake camp meeting. And now in this quiet solitude the sights and sounds and songs and fragments of conversation, and even the tones of individual voices, come floating back over my heart and mind, filling me with what dear Sister Mills calls "quiet hallelujahs."

Among many good things is the memory of the conversations and sermons of our venerable brother and chief pastor, Bishop Peck. Will we ever forget the narration of the simple and pathetic story of his early life and religious experiences. How after his conversion and entrance upon the ministry, when he allowed the subject of personal holiness to take hold upon him, when he would for weeks and months study about and pray for Christian purity, he observed that during those seasons, his whole soul, his experience and perception of spiritual truth were wonderfully quickened, and that when he allowed his personal interest in holiness to subside, there was a coldness and deadness that crept over his entire religious life. The remark struck me with force, and I preserved it, for it so illustrated the truth of Wesleyan theology, that no converted soul can retain the clear sense of justifying grace without going on to perfection. I gathered from the bishop's conversation that he received sanctification at a camp meeting. He said that soon after he reached the campground, a good woman approached him and asked, "Dr. Peck, how long have you enjoyed perfect love?" He said the question pierced him to the heart, but he answered with a sorrowful honesty, "Sister, I have never enjoyed that blessing." She then began to exhort him saying, "Dr. Peck, you are appointed to lead the people of God on to perfection, and how can you succeed without having the experience? Let us covenant to pray that you may receive this perfect love." He replied, "Sister, you will have to go farther back than that, and we will have to pray that I may feel the need of it."

A short time after this, at the same camp meeting, he went into a prayer service and sat down so absorbed with his own soul that he seemed oblivious of all present. Putting his face between his hands, he whispered to God that God would give him a broken and contrite heart, that he might weep. He cried,

"O God, give me tears!" Instantly, the great deep of his soul was broken up, and he wept freely. In this frame, he began composing mentally a sermon on the text, "We have not an High Priest that cannot be touched with the feeling of our infirmities," and while drinking in the fullness of that Scripture, the cleansing blood did its work. Soon after, he met the sister that was praying for him. He said to her, "I have new and strange feelings, and I want you to tell me what has happened to me." She looked him in the face and simply replied, "It is all right." (Oh, that hundreds of doctors of divinity in these philosophic days would let some meek and holy woman lead them to the purifying fountain!)

I wish the whole of the bishop's story could have been preserved verbatim and put into the hands of all young Methodist preachers, that they might be aroused to seek this internal heaven of heart purity in their early ministry. The bishop preached two sermons at the camp meeting, one on the fullness of righteousness, the other on the fullness of love. His first sermon on the hungering and thirsting after righteousness was full of strong Wesleyan theology. In the midst of this sermon, he said this: "The only way to personal holiness is to so hunger for it that you cannot live without it. You must so hunger for it that no one can draw or buy you away from it. You must feel the hunger biting your very soul. I know what that hunger is. It is not the appetite of a backslider or of an egotist, but the true born child of God that feels this need and hunger for holiness."

Again he said: "If you seek holiness, and in a short time give the pursuit up, you did not hunger and thirst. If you seek it at the camp meeting, and go home to be a persecutor of holiness, you did not get in the limits of this text; you did not thirst. You must get it strong! If I knew how to put it any stronger, I would."

Again: "You may think the preacher is severe with you. You may think he is cutting you to pieces, but it must be done. Your pride must be broken! Your will must submit, before the cleansing blood can reach you. You must be crucified. I am not one of those who try to make salvation easy."

In speaking of being filled, he said, "Quick as the flash of the eyes, when faith apprehends the power to save fully, the soul is filled. And when the soul is filled, then all this non-sense about there being no difference between regeneration and sanctification is swept away from the mind."

On our journey we fell in with Rev. J. S. lnskip and his wife, Rev. J. A. Wood and his wife, and a host of others, all enroute for the camp meeting.

Brother Inskip, the commander-in-chief of the camp, never seemed more filled with the heavenly Spirit. There were about one hundred and twenty-five ministers in attendance. Great numbers of them and their wives obtained the great pearl of heart purity. It was truly an old fashioned, orthodox, Methodist scene—to see presiding elders, ministers with their wives, local preachers, Sunday school superintendents and teachers, laymen rich and poor, all kneeling in the straw, and in the language of our discipline, "groaning to be made perfect in love in this life." Bowing with these were those seeking the new birth, from the gray-headed old man to the infant scholar. Oh, that such scenes were more common in our churches and at our camp meetings! There were about one hundred con-versions and over a hundred sanctifications at this meeting. It is a fact in harmony with the Bible that those meetings held directly for the promotion of holiness have more conversions of sinners than any other meetings, and the work is likely to be far more thorough and enduring.

The great Northwest is probably the most soul-expand-ing, heart-inspiring country on the globe. That country has an immeasurable history before it, and if we can contribute in planting the grand old Wesleyan doctrines and experiences of Bible holiness in that soil, we will do much for the answer of "Thy kingdom come." —G. D. Watson

CHAPTER 12

Goes Abroad

IN the summer of 1891, a party consisting of Dr. William McDonald and wife, Rev. Joshua Gill and daughter, and Rev. John A. Wood and wife, planned an evangelistic tour to England. Rev. Wood, who lived in southern California, decided about ten days before the time they had expected to sail that he could not go.

The other two workers felt the need of some strong helper to fill the vacancy.

Dr. Watson's slate was already filled until late in the autumn and winter. However, they urged him to cancel those engagements for the months he should be abroad, giving as a reason for it that the English work was most important at that time, and that he could easily secure substitutes for his home engagements.

After taking a few days to think and pray over the matter, he consented to their request; but it was too late to catch the ship, *Teutonic*, on which they had hoped to sail from New York.

It was early in September when the party of six steamed out from Boston harbor on the ship *Pavonia;* and the boat being a slow one, they were ten days reaching Liverpool.

As they stood upon the deck and watched the city grow smaller and the various objects become mere specks in the distance, Dr. McDonald turned away and remarked, "Now we are in for it."

Neither he nor Mrs. McDonald were good sailors. Although the trip was free from high seas or storms, yet they were much of the time in their staterooms. The others enjoyed the deck life and the dining room. But when they returned in November on the steamship *City of New York,* which was one of the largest afloat at that time, the old ocean was in a rougher mood. They all kept their staterooms until the storm was over; and after the sun shone brightly, the seas were very high. The chairs were tied to prevent them from slipping and sliding about the deck. Most of the way was rough and they were all glad to be back in the homeland once more.

For some months previous to going, Mr. McDonald and Mr. Gill had been corresponding with the various Methodist churches in England concerning this trip and had made engagements for several meetings in as many cities and towns.

The first meeting, however, was for ten days at Shipley with the Primitive Methodists.

They were cordially received and the congregations were excellent. There were results from the very beginning of the meetings, showing that the church was in a good condition for revival.

Many English customs were very awkward to the Americans, and they were wholly unprepared for some of them. They could not understand at first why the visiting ladies should be seated at the back of the church. It was explained afterwards that the best people occupied those seats. When they rent the pews they were a higher price.

At that time the system of travel was a constant surprise to them. Mr. Gill was delegated by the other members of the party to be responsible for the luggage, as the railroads did not check anything. The conductor locked them in until they were to change cars. Hence when the train stopped, Mr. Gill had to ask to be released so that he might attend to his duties.

When the train reached Shipley, imagine his surprise to find that his own traveling bag, which contained his essentials for Sabbath, was missing. It finally was restored to him the following week.

The people were extremely cordial and vied with each other in taking their guests over the beautiful Yorkshire hills to places of renown, when the meetings were suspended on Saturdays. Old Bolton Abbey was among them.

From Shipley they went to London for two weeks, then to Manchester, and on to other engagements until the allotted time was filled in. The following year Dr. Watson received a call to go over to the Easter services conducted by Mr. Crossley in Manchester. He accepted this and we remained nearly all summer.

There are a number of consecrated men in England that hold their membership in the various evangelical churches who long to see evangelistic meetings and efforts for the salvation of the masses. They are not called to preach themselves, consequently they are led to continue in their secular callings and provide money to support a mission and a competent man to work under their direction.

Mr. Crossley's work at Manchester, Mr. Reader Harris' work in London, and Mr. Myers' work in Bradford belong to this class; and they have the largest missions of that kind. The first two men have passed away, but their works endure. With these and several others of a similar kind, Dr. Watson labored during his second visit to England. One meeting at Colwyn Bay, Wales, we cannot forget. Mr. Crossley secured several workers and paid expenses of all travel and entertainment during the time. This meeting was in the Wesleyan Methodist Church.

In England or her colonies we have no Methodist Episcopal Church. There are various forms of Methodists, but none have bishops. The Established Church has the bishops.

The Wesleyan Methodists occupy in England the standing of the Methodist Episcopals here in this country, only they are more formal; but they still hold to the local preacher and give him a place for exercising his gifts, but no bishops.

We found also that when the English take a stand for God, the lines are more marked with regard to the Sabbath and matters of dress and temperance. We found as we mingled with the people, that no matter how much they possessed of the wealth of this world, if they were out-and-out for God, they would walk miles to church services rather than have their coachman or chauffeur absent himself from his worship in order to serve them. If they had guests and were obliged to accommodate them, they much preferred to call a public carriage. They were embarrassed to have their own seen upon the street because of the example on the Sabbath day.

As regards to temperance at that time among the better classes, a hostess was considered to have neglected her guests if wine was not served at dinner. A prominent Christian worker and member of the Established Church brought Dr. Watson and wife an invitation to dine with her mother, who lived a few doors from where they were staying. She said, "You must not be astonished if wine is offered you at dinner, for my mother would feel she had not treated you with courtesy. You turn your glasses down. That will avoid any trouble, and it will not be offered." The mother had not taken the stand for God which her daughters and household had, for they had banished it utterly.

Mr. Crossley and wife, who had cablegrammed Dr. Watson to come, were very thoroughly consecrated people. He was an exemplary church member and walking in the light of justification when one day he was passing along the street and stopped to listen to the testimony of a Salvation Army worker in a street meeting. The testimony was a clear one to heart purity.

Mr. Crossley was impressed with it and believed and received the definite experience. From then he was all for Jesus, and Mrs. Crossley took the same decided step. They together worked in the Master's vineyard from that time on.

He purchased an old downtown theater in the slums of Manchester, which he removed, and had erected upon the same location the present Star Hall Mission building, which was thoroughly equipped for the accommodation of his family and a necessary body of workers for all purposes of mission work in all its forms for that locality. But his efforts were not all spent there. He was interested and his money was used to help the needy and for the salvation of souls wherever he found them, whether through the Salvation Army, or to relieve the persecuted Armenians. Star Hall was then and is today a lighthouse in Manchester.

Mr. Reader Harris was well known as a member of the Queen's Council and barrister in the House of Lords, yet he owned and operated a mission, Speke Hall of London. It was in this mission that Dr. Watson reached the slums of London in the evenings, and in the afternoons there were drawing room meetings held in his home at Clapham Common, where more than a hundred came to hear the Bible readings. These were the gentry and ladies brought there by special invitation from Mrs. Harris each day. There were no idle spectators but eager partakers of the bread of life. Mrs. Harris assisted her husband with the publication of their paper, the *Tongues of Fire*, and did not hesitate to take her musical instrument and assist at the street meetings.

Mr. Meyers, of Bradford, also Mr. Walker, of Leicester, had similar missions, which we visited and in which we conducted some services. Dr. Watson was also engaged to preach in Exeter Hall and in Free Trade Hall to thousands of people. The closing services with Mr. Meyer at Bradford were a wonderful time of refreshing. About sixty were saved.

While at Garforth visiting Mr. Wooley, we rode over to Micklesfield to see the old home of the "Village Blacksmith," Sammy Hicks. His grandson, Watson, lives in the same house, and we were shown the old Bible and tall clock, which was still keeping good time. The old windmill was not far away, of which he tells us in his book.

We visited many other towns for one or two meetings each.

The last service was held at Star Hall by Dr. Watson and Mr. Brown of the Established Church of Liverpool, the theme of the sermon being, "The Promise of the Father." A most excellent after service was held.

The next day, July 16, 1892, we shipped on the S. S. *Gallia* for home.

In 1900, Dr. Watson and wife made an evangelistic tour to Jamaica, the Pearl of the Antilles.

We found an open door there in the Wesleyan Methodist Churches, through the agency of Mr. Hopkins. The people lifted from slavery through the instrumentality of Wilberforce of England, less than a hundred years ago, have been well evangelized, and have churches all over the island. The population is composed of all shades of brown, from the black to the lightest shades, with blue eyes. The clergy is also colored.

The whites there are missionaries or descendants of former Christian workers, and commercial men and families.

We visited several mission schools. One was composed of East Indian children, as their parents are brought here to labor. Another school taught by people from America was that of domestic science. We visited one mission on a mountainside. The missionary and his family were comfortably situated in a very neat home and were happy in their work. They were supplied with many luxuries from the States. The man and his wife were both from Canada. It was very rare to see a white face in their audience. He had other preaching places, and his parishioners came to him to settle their family and neighborhood disputes; and they never failed to abide by his decision.

These missionaries were deeply consecrated. Truly they had left all for Christ.

Later, when in Canada, we visited her mother's home. It was a veritable palace. To her it was a constant crucifixion to have her daughter in far off Jamaica struggling with the crude ways of doing things and no companionships as in her former home.

Jamaica, being a colony of England, is supplied with fine roads of stone. The natural scenery is the finest of all the countries we have visited.

R. J. Watson, brother of Dr. Watson, being the manager of the Philadelphia Line of United Fruit Company's Steamers, made it possible for Dr. Watson and his wife to have this magnificent trip to Jamaica twice.

E. Hopkins, an official of the company, who was in sympathy with Christian work and anything for the betterment of the island, entertained the couple at Port Antonio in that American Hotel, a poem of itself and a dream of beauty, with its location by the sea near the harbor, its wondrous soft climate, its wealth of flowers, its tropical fruits, and soft-voiced inhabitants. It was a blessed opportunity to work for God among that needy people, and we accepted every open door from one end of the island to the other during the weeks we remained.

We feel that this writing would be incomplete should we fail to record our stay of ten days at Bowdoin.

Captain Baker, of the United Fruit Company, with his lovely family, has his home at this seaport, where the boats come in for bananas and coconuts. A small church has been erected in the little town, and it was here that Dr. Watson preached each night during his stay in this locality. Captain Baker's office was at Port Antonio, where the American boats come in; hence he could only spend his weekends at lovely Bowdoin with his family. As his wife was a longtime invalid, he brought her here, with her son and daughter, and located them on this lofty eminence that she might enjoy the sunbaths of this tropical climate, undisturbed by the rigors of a New England winter or molested by the roaring city.

His dwelling, an old stone house of Spanish style with a large sun porch, was at the top of the hill, which gently sloped to the sea. Here were planted thousands of coconut and other trees, which did not intercept one's vision, but enhanced it. As one looked from the mansion house the vision swept over the tree-tops to the ocean beyond for many miles, where the ships were passing to and fro.

In order to entertain their friends he had erected several cottages suitable to the climate and adapted for small dormitories, around the brow of the hill a few rods from the main dwelling. The large drawing room and dining room were in there. Everything for comfort was prepared in every possible respect.

In a small enclosure not far away were the gentle deer looking up for a kind word or a loving pat. In the various cages were the parrots, and out in the trees the mocking birds.

Best of all, Captain Baker was a God-fearing man and had so trained his family, who were gentle, educated, refined, and Christian. On Sunday evenings, as his custom always was, he gathered the family about the piano with song books and, after the singing of songs that the mother liked, her preference was given for a sermon which was read from *The Christian Herald.* After prayer, commending them all to the keeping of his whose eye never slumbers, he said goodbye as if it were his last; and he was gone for another week. What a benediction to have such a husband and father, and what a privilege to have this man for president of the company!

CHAPTER 13

A Call to New Zealand

NEW Zealand on the map is very diminutive but, in reality, it is twelve hundred miles from north to south; and the beautiful scenery, of which so much has been written, is distributed over this territory. The hot lakes, wonderful geysers, boiling pools of mud, and terrace formations are in the Rotorua district, one hundred and forty miles south of Auckland. The magnificent Kauri forests are in the north, and the lovely Wanganui River is in the southwest region of North Island.

The Maoris still live along its shores and add greatly to the interest of the fascinating scene. Their carved houses are triumphs of savage art. The entire outside of the building is one mass of carving, all done by hand with knives. The designs are all similar, and mostly hideous faces with mouths open and tongues protruding. I suppose there is some reason for this; possibly they are to represent their heathen gods at one time.

Many of these natives are poor and indolent. Others who were wiser and kept their lands are now reaping the benefit and enjoy the comforts and luxuries of Europeans. But they still love the old manner of living; and although some build nice European houses, they prefer to squat on mats in a hut nearby than to live in their nice house and keep it. They live mostly in the open air; and some of their houses are built without door or window, simply a small opening down by the floor through which they crawl. These are used for sleeping.

One of their customs has been to tattoo their faces in curves and lines. Especially their chiefs, and the women, when married, have the mouth tattooed and colored dark in crooked lines down the chin. These people are now being evangelized, and have been for a number of years; and these old customs and habits of living are slowly passing away.

They are naturally socialists and use with freedom the property of another Maori, but not of the Europeans.

When one of their people dies, a trumpet summons the people from round about, who come and feast and continue to remain until everything like food is exhausted. Thus it is very hard for one to rise above his more indolent fellows.

If a Maori remonstrates against having his property used or destroyed, he is considered very mean.

They are a very affectionate, kind-hearted people, and generous to a fault. Mr. Gittos, the Wesleyan missionary who has been among them for many years, tells many interesting and some pathetic stories of them. They venerate him and love him as a father, or a great chief, and will obey him in nearly everything; and in perilous times, he has influenced them and made peace when no other power could do it. He tells of a mother bringing her darling baby to him as a thank offering. She had nothing else to bring, and she wanted in some way to express her gratitude and love for the missionary. He appreciated her kindness and told her that he would let her take care of the baby for him. This, of course, pleased her very much.

The climate of New Zealand is fine, and is the Mecca for England's suffering ones with throat and lung trouble. In the north there is never ice or snow, yet the summers are not extremely hot or depressing.

March is the first autumn month, yet it is much pleasanter than our American Septembers, and more like October. The air is very bracing. The flowers never know when winter comes, it is so mild. It is all summer to them, and they go right on blossoming. What a good time the children have playing out of doors with never a fear of serpents in the grass or shrubbery!

In the south they have ice and snow in winter, but the cold is not severe. The grandest of New Zealand's scenery is to be found in the South Island in the Southern Alps, where Mt. Cook lifts its snowy head, with glaciers streaming down its sides into the valleys.

In New Zealand women have had an opportunity of proving how much their votes can accomplish. The only saloons allowed here (in 1905) are the bars in hotels, and war is being waged against these with the hope of having temperance hotels only. In some parts this has succeeded.

They were far in advance of us in the United States then; but in 1927 we met some delegates from there at the great temperance convention in Los Angeles, and they reported that the States have outstripped them since.

After the age of sixty-five, those who have lived here twenty-five years receive a pension, if needed. To be sure, it may not exceed two dollars per week, but that is a good sum to one utterly destitute.

We have said elsewhere that the climate is a Mecca for suffering ones from Great Britain, but not all go for the sake of health. For various reasons they have immigrated to that English colony. One English gentleman, a member of Parliament for a number of years, moved all his large family there in order to settle them in country homes. He was a fine Christian. One physician from the South of London who was in ill health, and who had lost his voice, fled to New Zealand where he recovered his health, but not his voice. He had a fine practice there.

In another home we met an Irish lady who was in moderate health. She filled her place in the church work and in society. She told us that when she left Ireland her physician gave her only a few months at most to live, and that had been fifteen years before. They nearly all refer to some part of Great Britain as home. The nearest route is by way of America.

Having heard of the needs of New Zealand through others who had engaged in evangelistic work there, it was laid upon the heart of Dr. Watson to go when the opportunity offered. Mrs. Phelps, who had spent some years with her husband in that far away colony, related with much enthusiasm the success of those years among such a willing class of people and always with a desire that he should go there. The opportunity did not come until a few years ago.

On January 12, 1925, Dr. Watson *and* wife left San Francisco for New Zealand and Australia, to be absent for one year. This included a visit of six weeks in Honolulu and a short stop at the island Tutuilla, one of the Samoan group which belongs to the United States. It is the only foot of land possessed by the American government south of the equator and the spot where Louis Stevenson died and was buried. Dr. Watson had been in correspondence with several Christian people in New Zealand, and through these his first engagement was in Auckland with Central Mission. This mission is very much alive and has a constant revival. Mr. Smith, who opened this work and is the superintendent, took his first lessons in the old Jerry McCauley Mission in New York. He has wonderful tact for winning souls and is quite benevolent. He is one of the largest merchants in this city, but his business never seems to interfere with that mission work. It is a strong one and very aggressive. The choir, a large one, was accompanied with piano and several other instruments; and the singing was an inspiration. The building was commodious and well filled from the beginning.

Many active young people in this work are becoming established and making first-class workers. The people received us with beautiful hospitality. Souls were saved and cleansed at all the services.

After consulting the interested Christian workers and preachers as to his next move, Dr. Watson heeded their advice to go south as the winter was approaching and hold the next meeting at Dunedin, then work his way north and let Auckland, as it was the farthest city north, be open for his work in the winter.

Calls were coming in from the Wesleyan Methodists and Primitives, also the Baptists, and for union meetings of all the churches at other places. Eight months were blessedly used of God, in the salvation of souls and sanctification of believers, as they worked in Dunedin, Christchurch (a city), Wellington the capital, and many towns smaller and interior, and then went back to Auckland. These were all excellent, but we will give a glimpse at Waihi and another at Auckland.

The largest gold mines are at Waihi. It is quite a town, nicely built, having churches and halls and a good class of people there. There is also the rough element, which is always found in mining regions; but God adapts himself and his methods to all classes and makes the way of salvation equally plain to all, if they only listen to his voice.

A worker led to the altar a man who was regarded a hardened sinner. He had attended the church services there before the meeting, but had never been known to take a step towards God, and gave no one any cause to imagine that he had a conscience. He said to her, "I've tried so hard to live right, but I've failed. I can't do it." She told him that Jesus could save him and cause him to live right, also that Jesus was his best friend and loved him, even while he was sinning against him, and wanted to save him. He looked up into the face of the worker and said most pathetically, "You see, I never knew that before." It was not many moments until he was on his feet and said that Jesus did forgive his sins. One woman said, "I would sooner have gone without sixteen meals than to miss that Bible reading I've just listened to."

Here is an extract from one of the daily papers of Waihi concerning the revival there:

> Some of the wildest characters in the town have become changed persons. The churches are crowded and meetings are held all day and every day and in every place. It is quite a common thing to see a band of young fellows meeting in the street to sing and pray and speak. The miners hold prayer meetings underground. Meetings are held in the drives and on the sides of the hills. There is not the slightest trace of sectarian bitterness to be found there now. They all have too much to do. All the feeling there ever was has been completely broken down.
>
> It was a wonderful sight to see great, rough miners in tears; and it was remarkable to hear the testimonies from all over the hall, of persons who, there and then, resolved to abandon a life of sin and to henceforth serve their Master. The whole thing

seems to be in the air, and you cannot escape its influence if you would.

I should not be surprised if it were but the mere kindling of a fire in Waihi, which will sweep like a purifying blast right through the colony.

When the evangelists went to Waihi in August to hold a mission of ten days with the Wesleyan Church, they had secured the large Miners' Hall for the services and members of the various churches came to the meetings, the Baptist pastor being in full sympathy and taking an active part.

We found there two young men, neither of them twenty-one years of age, who had received sanctification and were fully baptized with the Holy Ghost six months previous to their coming. The young men had been giving brave testimonies and living beautiful lives. The persecution to which they had been subjected only polished their armor and they shone the brighter for God.

As Dr. Watson poured out the truth on sanctification, eyes and hearts commenced to open, and the yielding began among the prominent and best church members. As is always the case, and has been since the days of Pentecost, the revival started with sanctification of believers. It seemed a hard pull for several days, but a few were coming out into the light each day; and a large number of children and young people had come to Jesus the first Sabbath. We found in many places in New Zealand a shrinking from preaching on everlasting punishment, and many are drifting off into the belief that there is no such thing.

On the second Sabbath evening Dr. Watson took up the subject definitely and preached on the fixedness of character and on everlasting banishment from God.

The break came that evening. People rushed to the altar until it was filled. Some who did not seek the Lord went away angry and full of debate. The next day, the closing day of the meetings, we were told that there had never been such a stir in Waihi as that sermon had made, and that the town had been in commotion all day.

That same evening, the last of the evangelists' meetings, the altar was full of seekers; and the pastor of the Wesleyan church announced that the meeting would continue with the help of the Baptist ministers and others. Already one hundred and twenty had sought the Lord definitely. A letter from a friend a few days after reported two hundred had been reached, and still the number was increasing. The report had gone out over the colony, and ministers were coming in to see the marvelous effects of a genuine revival. It was to be similar to the Welsh revival a few years previous.

After the Waihi meeting, Dr. Watson and wife, having an engagement in Ashburton, reached there on Wednesday. Mr. Salter, the pastor, had arranged for the friends to call the next day and form their acquaintance. Among them were representatives of the town and also of the various churches. Among other testimonials of welcome our United States flag was suspended from the gallery of the church by the side of the New Zealand flag, which is the Union Jack having the Southern Cross on the blue. The pastor was in the enjoyment of full salvation; and things seemed in shape for a good meeting, which was realized in the next ten days.

We came in touch with many choice spirits while in the colony. While at Dunedin we came in contact with a business firm who sets aside a large percent of its income for the Lord. When the firm was young it began with the tenth. As it prospered, a larger percent was set apart. Then again it prospered yet more, and the Lord's share was greatly increased. At last accounts they gave twenty-five percent of their earnings. It kept books for God, as their senior partner, and was always ready to disburse the money in cases of need. At the end of the year the balance was divided and sent out to worthy objects, such as orphanages, pastors of weak churches, and for help of the aged and helpless. This firm expressed no desire to accumulate wealth.

The laws of that country regulate the business in such a way as to protect each man and give him an equal chance with all others of the same occupation. If there is an oversupply for the demand, then one firm must cease its business and shut up for a stated time, then open again and another close.

The firm I have spoken of, which had the Lord for its partner, had to abide by the law; hence, although they made a first class commodity (which all others did not), they must cease to continue when the law said so, even if the people demanded this brand. Regardless of this handicap, the firm prospered.

To go back a little in our story, during the first few days of his visit in Auckland, Dr. Watson, while out riding with a friend, passed the Baptist Tabernacle, which is rather an imposing building and able to seat from one thousand to fifteen hundred persons. He admired the church and remarked, "I would like to hold a series of meetings in that while here." It was simply a passing thought and not an expectation.

After conducting only two meetings in that city, a call came from Dunedin at the extreme south. The advice of his friends at Auckland was to go to Dunedin at that time. Being south of the equator, the north is warmest.

There were no lines of railway through from Auckland to even Wellington, the capital, much less to Dunedin; hence the correct way to travel would be by boat. He and his wife took the steamer around, taking some days to reach Dunedin. From there his engagements took him to the various towns and cities which have been mentioned.

A call came from the Baptist Tabernacle before the end of the eight months. After that he closed the tour in Smith's large mission where he began at first. A wonderfully successful tour it proved it to be. More calls were coming in from other parts of the colony, but the time now had come for closing here and going over to Australia.

The meeting in the Baptist Tabernacle proved to be the largest and most far reaching of any work in Auckland. The work which had been done in the other missions and churches in this city had prepared the people for this one.

The pastor had needed a rest; and now, while he should have a supply in the evangelist for two Sabbaths and the intervening week, he excused himself and took a leave of absence, with the consent of the official board. The first Sabbath was a marvel. Everyone seemed just waiting for an opportunity to take a public stand for Christ.

The Sunday school was turned over to the evangelists. After an address on "Deciding for Jesus," the opportunity was given for them to come forward. They came almost en masse. The officers and teachers were greatly edified and uplifted in their experiences, and encouraged when they witnessed the answers to their prayers for the salvation of their various classes.

The pastor was called back home to participate in this gracious visitation from God to his church. He said he had never witnessed anything like it, as he stood in his pulpit and looked over the crowded church and saw the various ones he knew so well deliberately rising in the galleries and, from all over the building, coming to the front to seek the Lord in conversion or perfect love. We shall never know until the day of reckoning what great things were accomplished in those ten days. That one meeting was worth the trip to New Zealand.

The week following the close of this meeting, the time had arrived when the evangelists should leave for Australia.

The strongest ties are often formed in meetings of this kind because they are spiritual.

A large company of these hot-hearted people, among them Dr. ----, the pastor of the Tabernacle, with several other ministers, assembled at the pier to say goodbye.

The American consul was there with his flowers and his good wishes. His good wife was very ill at that time. Her friend had come one day for Mrs. Watson to call upon her, saying she was very homesick and perhaps to see one from the homeland, although a stranger, would cheer her.

She was allowed to see but few friends and then only for a short time. The attending nurse watched the hands of the timepiece and informed one when it was time to leave.

With many tender memories of their stay in the colony and amid the handshaking and farewells, the evangelists boarded the ship and settled down for a *bon voyage,* although it was a little rough crossing the Tasman Sea.

With great pleasure we remember the six weeks in Australia, its open doors for work, the wholehearted welcomes, the pleasant hospitality, and Sydney with its wonderful harbor.

We trust much good was accomplished while in the various meetings there. These are great countries and worthy of a much longer tour than had been given, but circumstances forbade a longer stay. Dr. Watson thought then he would return, but he did not. After the war it was difficult to do so.

Brother Parker at Auckland urged a return and Dr. Watson endeavored to go, but was hindered in securing a permit in time. His ticket was purchased and he started, going as far as San Francisco, from which port his ship sailed while he was left still waiting to hear from Washington.

This rather surprised him, and for a time he failed to understand the providences of God in this; but his nearest friends realized his physical weakness and felt that this was God's appointment in compassion that kept him at home.

His wife had accompanied him in all his trips abroad and assisted in many ways in the meetings; but when he went to Japan, she was hindered, but willingly submitted to this, knowing he was in the line of duty.

In 1914, Dr. Watson accompanied Brother Charles Cowman and wife to Japan and also Korea. His mission was to preach to the young ministers. We have no written account of his work there. Mrs. Cowman said she was greatly impressed by his sermons and Bible readings, and she thought she never heard his like.

The World War broke out and he felt uneasy to be away so far from home, hence he returned sooner than he had expected. Some of his last work was done in Los Angeles at the Japanese Mission.

As we take a mental bird's eye view of these various countries and the thousands of souls touched by the sermons and the words spoken in conversation, during the time, we see by faith a host, coming up in that Great Day, who will testify they are among the number who rejoice in the fact they gave their hearts to the Lord, or learned the way more perfectly, during those meetings.

They will cast their crowns at Jesus' feet, and crown him Lord of all.

During the stay in New Zealand we did not attend any native service except a funeral of a noted old chief. He had known the days of cannibalism, but he had long since turned from this. Forsaking his own people, he joined the English Army and assisted in subduing the natives. At his funeral he was honored by both sides. Two ministers, in different languages, the English and Maori, officiated.

The custom among the natives, as in other such countries, is to honor the illustrious dead with burial on a hill. Only the preachers and the pallbearers ascended the very steep hill. The audience stood around upon the various elevations of land, which accommodated several hundreds, mostly Maoris. It was very weird and impressive when the band played "Abide With Me" as it reverberated among the hills.

After "Taps" had sounded and the actors descended the hill, the people stood about in groups over the immense area. The steam was rising from the hot springs, for this was at Rotorua, and the air was filled with fumes of sulphur.

Just when all was quiet, a woman slowly approached the foot of the hill, then stood with head thrown back, and gave a most piercing, bloodcurdling wail, which sends the shivers through the spine of the listener, making very real to him the passage, "He lifted up his voice and wept." After she had repeated this a few times, she retired to her bevy of friends and joined in the social conversation, while another mourner took her place.

They say these people are decreasing in numbers, and the time is coming when they will become extinct. Let us hope and pray that the Savior shall gather many jewels from among them for his crown.

CHAPTER 14

Work in Los Angeles

AFTER Dr. Watson had ceased to make Florida a winter home, it was hard for him and his family to adjust themselves to the cold winters of the east.

One season had been spent in California and he decided at that time to move his family there sometime in the near future. For many reasons it was thought best to take this step shortly after returning home from New Zealand.

We reached San Francisco, from Honolulu, in January, preceding the great earthquake there. Letters awaited their arrival, telling of serious illness with their children. Dr. Watson had engaged to do some evangelistic work in San Francisco, hence he remained to accomplish it, while Mrs. Watson hastened on to be with the sick ones in the east. Before another winter he had moved with his immediate family to Los Angeles. He believed that the children who were married would sooner or later follow, which they did, and also the unmarried one. They are now all comfortably settled and content in this land of sunshine.

Mrs. Watson had never entirely recovered from the effects of the grippe which she had before going to the islands of the Pacific. This had been followed by nervous exhaustion, and she never went on an extended evangelistic tour after returning from New Zealand. The ocean voyage was very beneficial, and the climate of California proved a boon to all the family. Dr. Watson could never say enough in its favor. However, when he made a home in Los Angeles, he had no thought of a settled mission work. This was suggested to him by his friends in the various churches of the city. At first he evangelized around the city in places nearby and sometimes supplied during the absence of pastors for a Sabbath.

When he had been here a few months, one of the Baptist pastors was going abroad to visit missions, and the church invited him to supply the pulpit in the pastor's absence. This he did for a few months, until the pastor returned, which proved very satisfactory. He now returned to his evangelistic work, but those who had attended his ministry felt there was a need for it in Los Angeles, and among themselves they talked and prayed that God might bring it about.

Finally, after seeing the way possible, they suggested it to him by letter, as he was away in meetings. He was getting to be quite well known here by that time; and if he was engaged for a meeting or a convention, the announcement that he would be there would ensure an audience.

Some years ago a Prophetic Conference was called in this city composed of various evangelical churches, it might be correct to say of all the evangelical churches, and one of the speakers failed to appear. His subject was to review a new book that only a few had yet read. The president of the meeting asked if anyone among those present on the platform had read the book and was willing to give a review of its contents. Some had read it, but were not prepared to review it. Hence no one responded.

Dr. Watson saw the dilemma. He promptly arose and said he had not seen the book, but he had formed some idea concerning its teaching from the remarks he had heard from others who had read it, and were capable of judging it. He was willing to give his understanding of it; and if he should err in his judgment, he was willing to be corrected as he proceeded.

It was interesting to watch the faces of those on the platform, the smiles of assent and nods of approval from those who had perused its pages. It was wonderful with what accuracy it was done, possibly better than it could have been done by the one to whom it had been assigned. He was always ready with an appropriate song or prayer and never indolent in the use of his gifts. When the suggestion to open such a meeting was made to him by his friends, he took time to think and pray over it.

Los Angeles was a great city and full of churches and missions of all kinds. If this was to be a successful meeting it must have something in it for the people that no other place had. This he well knew. And when he consented to the proposition, he laid himself out for it and was on his face before God day and night. He was noted for his originality, his enthusiasm, and his perseverance. These all served him well. His enthusiasm was contagious and his audiences partook of it. God had given him a personality that few possess, but he knew he could not lean on these things. He prayed and had faith that God could do it, and thus it was accomplished.

> Faith, mighty faith, the promise sees
> And looks to that alone;
> Laughs at impossibilities and cries,
> "It shall be done."
> In hope against all human hope,
> Self-desperate, I believe;
> Thy quickening Word shall raise me up,
> Thou shalt thy Spirit give.

When he went to New Zealand and Australia, he had not the means to pay his way back home. If he had broken down, and he had no home to which he could return, nor a bank account to meet his expenses, there was only one way to look and that was upward and onward by faith. We could not advise another to follow his example. It might be a failure for you, dear reader, without the requisite faith. The Lord had abundantly opened his way there and owned his work by crowning it with his blessing and given much success. Now surely God could give guidance in establishing this meeting and wisdom to carry on, with the support of those he had used to suggest it.

All must be according to the promptings of the Spirit. He realized he must lean on none but God. He listened to the counsel of his godly friends and sought to harmonize with their advice so far as it pleased God. "God helps those who help themselves," is an old maxim. It simply means, in Bible language, that he is a co-worker with his people. We are not to sit idly by and wait for God to do his part and ours too. We are to be the willing and ready instruments in his hands to accomplish his purposes.

After being convinced of the right course to pursue, through fasting and much prayer, he rented the best hall he could secure at that time, downtown, so as to reach the masses, and large enough to accommodate several hundred persons, and he preached on Sunday afternoons, lifting freewill offerings to meet expenses. There were no committees and no responsibility upon anyone.

Dr. Watson did not depend entirely on his audience to advertise the meeting, but each Saturday his notice appeared in the daily paper with the other places of worship. This meeting began well and often the house was filled to its capacity.

The audiences were composed of representatives of many of the churches in the city and beyond the bounds of the city, Burbank, Santa Monica, and Glendale, and the outlying towns round about. In addition to these were the tourists.

When Christian people come to Los Angeles, they very naturally look to Saturday's paper to inform themselves concerning the spiritual tables prepared for their enjoyment on the morrow, and choose the best for their participation.

Brother B- has just arrived on the morning train. He has only a few days in Los Angeles, and he wants to take it all in, if possible. As he searches the paper, he finally comes to the pages filled with every announcement conceivable of various meetings. He has heard of certain pastors and churches and feels desirous to hear all of them. But presently he comes to the notice of this new mission opened by Dr. Watson on the "Grand Old Doctrines of the Bible." He remarks to his companion, "Who do you think I have found on this column? None other than our dear old friend Watson, and his subject for tomorrow will be, 'Does God answer prayer?'"

She replies, "Surely we must take that in!" He cuts out the notice and slips it in his pocket, so he shall make no mistake about finding the place and be sure to get there on time.

The next day he and his wife attend a renowned church of excellent repute and hear a fine Scriptural sermon in the morning; but in the afternoon they wend their way to Hill and Fifth Streets. They reach the place early and get a choice seat. The people are coming in, and everyone seems so cheerful and happy, each speaking to the other. The hymnbooks are already on the seats. The piano is open, and everything is ready for the service to begin. The hall is quite well filled.

A young lady walks in and takes the seat at the piano. She is just from one of the churches, where she has attended the Sunday school and listened to a fine sermon from her pastor. Now she is over here to help in the music and enjoy the meeting. She is very alert, and a great asset to this meeting. Everyone listens to her touch of the instrument. She allows no dragging in the singing and sees that the congregation keeps time. The songs are well chosen and full of spirit and life. All engage in it as if their hearts are full of it, and their lives depended on making a joyful noise unto the Lord. Someone calls for, "Oh thou in whose presence my soul takes delight." As it is sung in the spirit, it is a balm to the heart. Another calls out, "Please sing, 'When the roll is called up yonder, I'll be there.'" They sing and look as if they are sure they will.

Dr. Watson enters before they sing the first hymn, and as he sings, his piercing eyes sweep over the audience. He recognizes the tourists and steps down from the platform to go welcome them. He cannot wait because something might hinder at the close. After the singing and prayer, the testimony meeting begins where it had left off a week ago. They all know that unless they are prompt, they will not be heard from.

"Iron sharpeneth iron; so a man sharpeneth the countenance of his friend." In this case the spiritual experience and utterance of one spiritually-minded man whets another's appetite for the spiritual. It becomes contagious. All who have a spark now become aflame. Everyone present seems to want to add his testimony, and it comes with a glow and warmth that only the Holy Spirit can give. The testimonies are to the point and not too long.

They have a victorious ring. Our friend tourist feels their fervor and power, and is soon on his feet, telling how God saved him and keeps him in the whirl and bustle of life. He praises God for leading him and his wife here today. He feels as if he were in the old Mountain Lake Park meetings or some great National, for the spirit is the same. He rejoices that God let him see the notice in the paper and says that he shall be glad to come again, if he is in the city.

The hour for the testimony meeting is nearing the close. Several are on their feet to speak, but the leader suggests that these testimonies will keep until next time. Preaching service begins on the hour. Those of our readers who have heard Dr. Watson preach at great camp meetings and elsewhere can imagine something of the sermon he preached from the subject announced. Often the call was given at the close for those seeking the Lord in any way. He kept a list of names and addresses of all who came to the meetings, including tourists. This became a permanent work. He spent about two years with it, then the evangelistic pull was on him again to other fields for camp meetings and summer work

During the years which he had been conducting this work he had been occupied in the studying and writing for the *Way of Faith* or *God's Revivalist,* also accepting any calls that came in between the Sunday work, such as answering calls to visit the sick, bury the dead, and even marrying couples when they came.

When the summer was over and Dr. Watson returned to his home, after resting a while he would look after the hall, to see if the same one he had before he left was available.

For three or four years, during the latter part of his life's services, he secured the S. S. Hall of the Temple Baptist Church near Central Park, a beautiful and large room with galleries. There was an elevator to reach it, as it was on the second floor. It was fully equipped with everything needful. It was located in the best place possible for such a meeting, downtown, only two blocks from the First Methodist Church, on two car lines, convenient to hotels and everything else that could be desired. He would fix the date and rent the hall, then go to his usual printer and have several hundred cards struck off, putting his photograph on them with the dates, location, and an invitation to come to the meetings and hear "the grand old doctrines of the Bible." Sometimes he would give his subject for the opening Sunday.

We have already stated that he had a list of all the names and addresses of his audiences. If new ones came in, as they always did each Sunday, he made it a point to speak to them at the close and take their address. Now he was prepared to send a card to each one individually, announcing his opening. The Saturday previous, he inserted a notice of the same in the church columns of the daily paper.

He prayed every day, and every step of the way, and looked to God to give him his audience. Of course it was there. The Holy Spirit was there in convicting power and in converting and cleansing hearts. Dr. Watson was in his seventies at that time, not quite so agile as he once was; but his mind was alert, and it was marvelous with what vigor he presented those saving truths. Sometimes he sat on a chair, when not feeling so strong, or leaned on the table for support; but his voice never failed him. The people loved him. They hung on his words; and often, when he was through, they gathered about him taking their turn in asking questions concerning the truth. On his return they always expressed much joy to welcome him back and told him how they missed his words of instruction during his absence. We are led to think *that* was one of the most fruitful periods of his life. Many were his fast friends here as elsewhere, and they never failed him in any way.

A short time before his release, we were both astonished when the mail brought data from the publishing house of the *Who's Who in America*, asking to have it corrected and returned at once or it would be printed in the book as it was. It was wisdom to correct some great mistakes in it and let them have it; so we did. Hence, his memory is perpetuated in that book, but not all that he did. Many of his books and other writings are not there. We tried to learn who had sent in his name for this book, but we failed to discover the party. Thus somebody was always doing some kindness and giving him cause for gratitude as long as he lived.

The people also loved his writings. He was possessed with vision and produced in his books something new, which God saw fit to use to reveal the possibility of a walk with God, to arouse the latent aspirations of any Christ-loving believer, and to show how to receive the Holy Spirit. With luxurious ease he liked to dilate on the Bible. He has now his reward for the defense of the gospel. The good that he did lives after him.

In 1892, while evangelizing with the Wesleyan Church in South Carolina, he decided to change his church relations, from the Methodist Episcopal Church to the Wesleyan Methodist. It was about this time that he accepted the premillennial coming of Jesus.

While in Florida recuperating from a nervous breakdown, it afforded him great relief to go to the woods where the quiet was perfect. While out there one day sitting on a log, wrapped in meditation, the Lord opened the Scripture to him on that subject and made it as plain as noonday. From that time he never had a doubt about it. It permeated his writings and sermons, and the last article he ever dictated was on the millennium.

Chapter 15

Last Days

DR. Watson's last evangelistic tour east was in 1921. When he went, he summoned all his strength to begin the journey and trusted day by day for new energy from on high. We persuaded him to wait until he should be improved, but he felt the call too strongly to resist it. His first meeting was at Syracuse, New York, with Brother Cox. Of this meeting the leader writes:

> Dr. Watson was an old fashioned full salvation preacher. He was preaching holiness and writing books and tracts on the second blessing while some of the younger giants were in swaddling clothes. Among his tracts were "The Two Crossings" and "The Indwelling Comforter." *White Robes* and *Holiness Manual* were among his first books.
>
> He was the evangelist at the first Syracuse camp, and his labors were made a blessing to the saints. We often hear someone refer to the meetings and the encouragement they were to them. At that time he was not well, and we feared he would not be able to continue to fill his part of the program to the close of the camp. His heart was in the work, his mind was clear and active, and his voice was strong; but his body was weak, and many of his messages were delivered as he sat in a chair. But the Lord strengthened and refreshed him, and he finished the meeting and went his way, preaching at several other camps and conventions before he returned to his home in California.

From this place he journeyed to North Carolina to attend the yearly camp which was held by Brother Compton at Asheville. He often spoke of the blessed time he had while there, and at other places on that trip.

105

We scarcely think he realized his work was near an end. Being wearied from travel on his homecoming, he thought that after a little rest and relaxation he would be able to take up his regular preaching once more; but as time passed on he did not improve sufficiently for any regular work. He held a few cottage meetings and gave some Bible readings at the Japanese Mission. Occasionally he preached for the pastor, Rev. Davis, of the Bible Tabernacle.

As time passed on, he grew feebler but was yet able to get out some. He delighted in listening to Rev. E. E. Helms of the First Methodist Church preach. He is a Bible student and a very forceful preacher, speaking with authority. Dr. Watson would lean forward and eagerly take in the sermon without ever taking his eyes from the speaker. When the sermon was ended, he always remarked to his companion, "He does not preach long enough." Not that he meant it as a criticism, but it was so enjoyable to him to hear such sermons that it gave him ideas. Thoughts were put in such clear utterances that he wanted to hear more. He would then walk up to the pastor and thank him, telling him how he enjoyed it.

No one knows the sad experience, except those who pass through it, of watching a loved one decline, seeing him grow a little weaker every day for three years, while every day we are trying to afford relief of some sort, but without avail. We took him to Santa Monica beach, taking a small cottage there, and letting our home in Los Angeles out to strangers. For a time he seemed better; and then again he declined until July 25, 1923, when he took to his bed and never again went around. Many friends came to see him and pray with him; but he said from the first that his work was done, although he had hoped to write a few more books. He suffered much pain in his feet, and also with that insatiable thirst that accompanies diabetes. Although at times his sufferings were intense, at others he was placid and very quiet. His sense of humor would now and then assert itself. When faint and weak, and when he needed to rise from his chair, he would say, "Brother Sampson, come help me up." One of his nurses came here from Texas and he called him "Short Hom."

Prayer was his main thought and occupied nearly all of his time. He often remarked, "Oh, that I could pray like Daniel prayed!" In the evenings we gathered in his room for Bible reading and worship. He always told us what to read, and when he was strong enough he would lift his voice and hands in supplication to God. These were precious seasons to all of us. His sleep was filled with dreams, and it was a common occurrence for him to say in the morning, "I was in another camp meeting last night. I was well and going among the people, speaking to them before I went into the pulpit to preach." In one of his dreams he was to preach on the "Fiftieth Psalm," "The Three Classes of Men." As he became more feeble, he grew almost impatient to "go home." One beautiful Saturday morning, he said, "Oh, if I could only go home today! I think it would be glorious to go to heaven on Saturday."

I said, "Wouldn't it be grand if Jesus would come and gather us away now before you go alone?"

He replied, "Oh, yes!"

All of these days he was receiving visits from his friends at intervals. Many of these friends he had not seen for years as they had just come out to the coast. They were always talking of God's work and he spoke to them of his going "Home," as if he were away and coming back to his home here. To a friend he said, "I have preached all I can and written all I can, and I cannot do any more. Tell the people my work is done."

When told that Brother Chrisman had returned from the north, he said, "Send for him. I want him to take charge of my funeral." In a few days Rev. Chrisman was here and received the instructions. The two had evangelized together eighteen years ago when first corning to this city. Again he said, at another time, "I am too weak to pray now except in my mind, and I am asking God to permit me to be conscious to the last, and that he may sustain and bless you." His sight was going fast. We prayed that the vision should continue to the end, and that his brain should not fail. Surely this request, too, was answered. A few days before he went, he said to a friend, "You have a good mother, and I have a good wife, and the kind Savior who is corning soon to take me Home, and I'll be so glad. Praise the Lord!" Again he said, "O Eva, the Lord has a great reward for you. It will be so great it will astonish you." From this time he lingered on the borderland as if sleeping. One of the pastors, Rev. McIntyre, came in; and as he, with the family, stood by the bed, I repeated in my husband's ear, "In my Father's house are many mansions. If it were not so, I would have told you. I go to prepare a place for you that where I am there ye may be also." He aroused, opened his eyes, and said, "Can it be I am going?" The answer was, "Yes, you are going now." Then he said, "I am so glad! Perfect peace!" When asked if he had any pain, he said, "Not an atom." A little later he said, "Are all here?" We assured him we were. The preacher talked to him and prayed with him, thanking God for a salvation that could enable him to triumph over death. A few hours later, he quietly gave a little sigh, and all was over. The battle is fought, the warfare is ended, and victory won, and he is Home at last. "Happy the spirit released from its clay!"

It is impossible to realize that his voice will be heard no more, nor will he return from trips as of yore, to be with the family in the home, and sing and pray and preach as he only could.

For about forty years he went up and down in this land preaching the gospel with gracious results. He also went to Canada, England, Jamaica, New Zealand, Australia, and Honolulu, his wife accompanying him to these places. His last trip abroad was to Japan, with Brother and Sister Cowman, where he was made a great blessing to the young workers in that field. His great work, at least in the latter years of his ministry, was instructing, building up, and feeding the saints with the richest spiritual food.

During these years he wrote fourteen books and, had his strength permitted, he would have continued to write.

In many things he had no equal. In fifty-four years his wife never tired of his preaching. The same sermon came always with freshness and a new unction. He was an affectionate husband, a kind father, and a faithful friend. It is only the consolation of the Holy Spirit that enables us to say, "Thy will be done," in a victorious spirit.

> Up to that beautiful city of light,
> Gathering Home, gathering Home;
> Up to that city where cometh no night,
> God's children are gathering Home.

The *Alliance Weekly* writes, "Dr. Watson was well known for his masterly sermons and helpful writings in periodicals and was the author of a number of books."

The funeral service was conducted by Rev. C. H. Chrisman, pastor of the Tabernacle in Glendale, California, who read one of Dr. Watson's sermons on "Heaven." Rev. George W. Davis, of Los Angeles, read an obituary, giving an account of Dr. Watson's life from the time he was converted in the Confederate Army. What a full life he lived! Rev. E. J. Richards, of New York, who was then in California, touched on a few of his experiences with Dr. Watson, first at New Castle, Pennsylvania, where Mr. Richards was then pastor in 1898, then in Los Angeles, in 1912, and in Asheville, North Carolina in 1921. Rev. Gates, pastor of the Methodist Church at Santa Monica, spoke of Dr. Watson's closing days.

Mrs. Watson, one daughter, Mrs. F. J. Kinder, and two sons, Rev. Fletcher Guard Watson, a member of the Southern California Conference, and George Cookman Watson, a lawyer of this city, and five grandchildren survive him.

Rev. John M. Pike, for many years editor of the *Way of Faith,* and who was in close fellowship with Dr. Watson covering a long period of years, says:

> I was frequently united with him in revival meetings. He had a strong personality and was fearless in his declaration of truth. He had a remarkable gift for illuminating the Scriptures and was unsurpassed as a Bible expositor. His style of preaching interested all grades of hearers, arresting the attention of the

unsaved, and imparting instruction and comfort to Bible students of all ages and conditions.

A friend who was present at the funeral penned the following lines to Mrs. Watson, descriptive of the occasion:

> How lovely the surroundings, as he lay there in that beautiful place looking so peaceful with the wonderful floral tributes about him! And how becoming that the leader should choose to read those inspiring thoughts on the "Joys of Heaven" from his own book! This surely illustrated, "He being dead yet speaketh."

How fitting that these ministers should be there and tell of his work and of their close association with him! Their words showed depth of thought, like the one they honored. They were settled, and knew whereof they spoke.

His body rests beneath the beautiful palms in Rosedale Cemetery in Los Angeles, awaiting the first resurrection.

Such wonderful tributes of love for him, as the letters expressed to me from those who have been saved and helped through his ministry, I have never seen! One brother says, "The ten days I spent in the meeting with him were 'days of Heaven on earth.'" I appreciate these many tributes more than I can express.

CHAPTER 16

"A Man Sent From God"

by Evangelist J. M. Hames

IN one of the gospels we read of "a man sent from God." He was "a burning and a shining light."

The above words could be applied to our beloved brother and friend, Dr. George D. Watson. Of all the preachers with whom it has been our privilege to associate, we have never met a greater than Dr. Watson.

There were several outstanding traits in his character that made him great. Among them we shall mention a few.

First, he was very deeply spiritual. There was nothing shallow, foolish, or superficial about his makeup or ministry. He was one man who practiced the presence of God continually. While he believed in and taught sanctification as a second work of grace, yet he never dreamed of stopping merely at being sanctified, but, like the holy Fletcher, his soul was on the stretch for all the fullness of God.

Dr. Watson taught and believed in a divine "ripeness," where all the fruits and graces of the soul ripen and mature for eternity. In his book, *Bridehood Saints*, in the chapter on "Signs of Ripeness," he says:

> The two most interesting periods in a fruit orchard are the times of blossoming and of blossoming and of ripening fruit. Some are more interested and attracted to the blossoming period when the orchards are dressed in white and pink, but the owner is more intensely interested in the ripening of the fruit and the amount of harvest. The same things are true as applied to the spiritual life.

111

There were certain marks in our brother's life that showed he was entering the state of maturity, such as a oneness with Jesus, to where his soul was constantly fed with the love of God. Everything hard and flinty had been crushed out of him by the deep crucifixion through which he had gone. His whole being seemed to be saturated in a divine sea of tenderness. There was a mellowness in his voice, a tenderness in his eyes, a refinement about his manners, showing that he had taken several courses in the school of obedience and suffering which had transformed him into a Christlike being.

He had faith without doubt, love without a trace of bitterness, humility without a touch of pride, gentleness without harshness, perfect courage without fear, the white heat of zeal without the touch of fanaticism, so that the graces of the Lord Jesus were poured into him and ran through him like a clear, limpid stream, without any earthly mud mixed.

Second, he was a man of prayer. Prayer was more to him than mere calling upon God. His soul was drawn out in intercessory prayer to where all the soul's faculties were under the divine sway of the Spirit. God seemed to take hold of the very fountain of his whole being like an infinite lodestone drawing out his desire, affection, and will into the current of divine intercession. In his own words let him tell us of some marvelous answers to prayer:

> I remember, one week in the early summer of 1885, that many different things were pressing sorely on my heart. The Holy Spirit put on me a burden of prayer which seemed greater than my heart could contain. After pleading with tears for several days, I cried out in agony, "O Lord, please put this burden of prayer on some of your dear saints to share this prayer with me!" In four days I received three letters in the same mail—one from the city of Denver, one from the hills of Kentucky, and one from a village in Georgia—each saying that on a certain day, the day of my agonizing prayer, they had been strangely and powerfully burdened in prayer for me, and all these three testified of having the assurance that the prayer would be answered. You can only imagine how the conjoint testimony

of these three letters—all received the same moment—went through my innermost heart. I have these wonderful letters yet, every one of them written as under direct inspiration of God. My poor heart swells with love and my eyes flow with tears of gratitude, and in memory I read over and over the life pages of marvelous, far-reaching, particular, personal and precious leadings of the blessed Comforter. The deeper our union with Jesus, the more clearly we recognize the presence of God in every thing and event.

We might say the secret of our brother's great life and ministry was his deep prayer life. Remember, deep spirituality and prevailing prayer are like the Siamese twins which cannot be separated.

Third, Dr. Watson was noted for being, even in his last days, an earnest, faithful student. So many, after passing a certain age, give up most all studies and rely upon past experience. Consequently they become dry and stale to the people. It was not so of our brother. There was a freshness about his messages that gripped the hearers.

Fourth, he was truly a great preacher. I question whether he had an equal in the entire holiness movement. His preaching was mostly of the expository nature. There was something about it that was simply impossible to describe. His messages not only gripped and held the people spellbound, but his words were loaded and pierced the hearts of the people like red-hot bullets shot out of a divine magazine. When he preached upon such subjects as "The Inner Life of Holiness," his words seemed to drip with power, sweetness, and glory. The people listened to catch every word. The fiery eloquence either evoked a smile or a flowing tear or awakened conviction.

We well remember at the great Cincinnati camp held on "The Mount of Blessings," when the bell boy would announce on the campground, "Dr. Watson's Bible Reading," you would see hundreds of people making their way to the tabernacle to get a seat near the front. When Dr. Watson got through with a text, there was no more to be said on the subject. Those passages never seemed the same again after he bathed them in a heavenly sea of light.

Fifth, one more thing that stood out in his life was his great books. There is something about Dr. Watson's books that will live forever. A great many religious books can be read once and they do not appeal to you again. Not so with his books. You can read them over and over and they grip and feed the soul and seem so fresh and new every time you read them. This writer has read his book, *Soul Food,* at least a score of times and yet we would not part with it, if we couldn't secure another one, for its weight in money. Every preacher in the holiness movement should have his nine great books. They cover every important subject in the Christian experience.

One more thought will be given about our beloved brother. He was a strong believer in the premillenial coming of Jesus. He often expressed his desire of being among the "caught-up ones" in the rapture, but God saw fit to take his tired servant before that time. We know that he will have the happy privilege of coming back with the Lord in the air to meet the "caught-up ones," and he will have a part in the first resurrection.

In conclusion I would say, let us who remain buckle the armor a little tighter and press the battle to the very gates of the enemy, and girdle the globe with full salvation in order that we might get the bride ready for the near coming of our Lord, and whether we live or die we will meet the Lord in the air with all the martyrs, missionaries, great preachers, and saints from all ages.

ARTICLES BY DR. WATSON

CHAPTER 17

A Thousand Years from Now

THE other evening while I was wafting my "goodnight" thoughts to Jesus, just before falling to sleep, the words, "A thousand years from now," seized upon my mind and wrapped me round for a few moments with the great calm realities of a blissful eternity. Almost intuitively my heart was filled with the following meditations:

Where will I be a thousand years from now? I am perfectly persuaded and assured that I shall never be annihilated but will exist in all the real properties of my being through all the coming eternal years. Even now, in this world, I am ever changing my locality in space, yet always occupying some point. I know that my conscious personality will be soon removed to some unexplored region of space. How soon will I fly from this spot! How soon will all the familiar surroundings of this world vanish like an ethereal dream from my senses, and I, who am now looking out of these eyes upon these words, stand and move amid new scenes in the distant parts of creation! My Bible tells me of a local paradise somewhere in my Father's dominion where the departed saints commune and rest with Jesus until the "great day." Beyond that, it tells me of a new heaven and new earth and of many mansions. When a thousand years have rolled away, by the grace of God, my conscious residence shall be amid those holy regions. In a few seasons those hidden realms will be as simple and as plainly real to me as the paper on which I see these words.

What will I be a thousand years from now? The question concerning my locality is not half so vital as this question about my character. I know within myself that moral configuration, spiritual character, is the pivot on which creation and the ages swing. One thing is fixed beyond repeal. That is, I will inevitably have some sort of character forever. What will it be? My personal interests and wellbeing a thousand years to come are just as real and important to me as those of the present moment. A thousand years to come I will still be I. I will feel, remember, reason, imagine, think, love or hate, hope, and believe. I shall never bid myself goodbye. I shall never get away from myself. Can God so harmonize myself with himself, so strike an interior chime in my soul that I shall never fret with myself, nor get tired of myself? What will I be? I do not know, but I am determined to let God make me just what he wants me to be a thousand years from now.

And if God, even my Father, has his blessed way with a poor thing like me for a millennium, oh, what infirmities he can smooth out, what awkwardness he can untangle, what cataracts of thought he can pour through my mind, what unfathomed streams of emotion can he turn on my heart!

What shall I see a thousand years to come? I will not be alone. I shall have some species of vision by which to apprehend beings and things that surround me. I shall see more really then than now. I shall see substances, not shadows. If I do not see colors, I will see the secret cause of all colors, which will be more real. On what vast and tranquil magnitudes will I gaze? Into whose countenances shall I look? What strange and multiplied acquaintances will I form in one thousand years from now? If I can gaze on the ascended Jesus of Nazareth, I shall not really need to look on others. If I do not look on him, then looking on all others would do me no good.

What will I do a thousand years to come? That will depend on what God wants me to do. To rest at his command is far better than to work when he commands not. I shall want to do just what the angels do, namely, his will, knowing that if it be action, I will never become indolent. A thousand years from now! It will surely come. I shall see it! Am I ready? Why not? I have the entire Bible, the entire atonement, the entire Holy Spirit offered to me. I will give up all and receive all. Yes, I will relax every thought of care, close my eyes, and lay me down to sleep on that hand which will bear me a thousand years to come!

CHAPTER 18

The Shepherd and the Sheep

Scripture Lesson: Psalm 23

The Lord is my shepherd, I shall not want. He maketh me to lie down in green pastures: he leadeth me beside the still waters. He restoreth my soul: he leadeth me in the paths of righteousness for his name's sake. Yea, though I walk through the valley of the shadow of death, I will fear no evil: for thou art with me; thy rod and thy staff they comfort me. Thou preparest a table before me in the presence of mine enemies: thou anointest my head with oil; my cup runneth over. Surely goodness and mercy shall follow me all the days of my life: and I shall dwell in the house of the Lord for ever.

I was preaching eighteen years ago in a big tent, and I announced that I would expound the twenty-third Psalm. A lady in the audience said to a friend, "I guess I will not come tomorrow, for I have heard so many sermons on that Psalm, and none of them have ever given me satisfaction." Her friend said, "Well, you have not heard this man explain it. Perhaps you had better come." So she came, and at the close of the address she said, "Well, your explanation of the twenty-third Psalm is absolutely satisfactory to my soul. I have been marvelously blessed."

I am going to give you just exactly what the Holy Ghost opened up to my mind on this Psalm. The Psalm is not a lot of beautiful words put together like fruit in a basket, in a tumbled-up way. It is an inspired picture of the steps that the believer takes in the spiritual journey from earth to Heaven. It is a clear description of the successive steps that we take from the new birth on to glory. That is why it makes no mention of pardon or repentance. It starts from the standpoint of the new birth and goes right on describing the progress of the Shepherd and the sheep.

In the first verse the original is "Jehovah is my shepherd." When Jesus says, "I am the good Shepherd," he identifies himself with the Jehovah of this same chapter. This is an invaluable proof of the deity of the Lord Jesus, and that Jesus Christ is the Jehovah of the Old Testament.

"Jehovah is my shepherd, I shall not want." The fact that Jesus Christ is God, and that we belong to him, and he is our Shepherd, gives us a perfect assurance that he will take care of us. There can be no mistake as to God's providence and his care of us as long as we have perfect assurance that he is our Shepherd. That assurance in the heart will dispel all doubt and all fear, for we have the consciousness that we belong to the Son of God. That does away with all misgivings.

The next step from the standpoint of the new birth is, *"He maketh me to lie down."* There we have a picture of a soul after being fed, lying down at the feet of Jesus. The very act of lying down indicates perfect contentment with God's will, a perfect and everlasting consecration to all his will. Sheep will not lie down if they are hungry or scared. But when they are well fed and free from all alarm, they lie down, in quiet and rest at the feet of the shepherd. This is a picture of entire abandonment of the soul to the Lord Jesus Christ, which comes after the new birth. We lie down at Jesus' feet, in the act of perfect consecration. We lay down all care and anxiety of the past and future—all the past, all the future, all we have, all we do not have, all we are, all we want to be, every thought, every plan, every ambition—we lay them down at the feet of Jesus Christ, that he may possess us, perfect us, guide us. A perfect consecration gives to God not only all we have, but all we are.

The next thought is about the "green pastures." "He maketh me to lie down in green pastures." The shepherd chooses the place where the sheep are to lie down. So Jesus Christ chooses all the program of our sanctification when he begins to work a great work upon the heart. He chooses the circumstances, the conditions. He provides that the hungry soul be led to some camp meeting or convention or holiness meeting, or he provides some good book or paper. If you watch in your lives, you will find God has a special providence not only on the outside, but on the inside. God chooses the place where you make a complete consecration, a place of green pastures. The soul must be well fed and in good condition in order to make a complete consecration. It is in green pastures, not stony ground, not desert land. The soul that makes a complete consecration is in green pastures. A backslider cannot make a perfect consecration.. A sinner cannot make a consecration. No one can make a complete consecration until be has a good religious experience.

"He leadeth me beside the still waters." The margin reads, "Waters of quietness." The still waters are a river, and that river is the Holy Ghost. When we make a complete consecration, then the Lord leads us to the river of the Holy Ghost. The Holy Ghost is given after we make a complete consecration. There is a river that is spoken of in various places throughout the entire Bible. This river with four heads is mentioned by Moses, David, Isaiah, Ezekiel, and John. First we read of it in Genesis, in the garden of Eden, and it runs on through the book of the Apocalypse, clear out through the New Heaven and the New Earth.

There are many emblems of the Holy Ghost in the Bible. The first emblem is the dove, then oil, and fire. But he is compared to a river more than all other emblems put together. The Holy Ghost is never compared to standing water, to a pond or a lake. He is compared to a river that flows, always in motion, never standing still, never stationary. He is from eternity to eternity, never beginning, never ending, and a sweet, divine, holy, heavenly, supernatural outflowing from the heart of God the Father. And so the Scriptures reveal that the Holy Ghost is a river that flows out of the sanctified heart, a divine stream that never stops but flows on forever from the heart of God the Father:

"He restoreth my soul." Now most everybody thinks that means the backslider in the church. It may include the backslider, but

that is not the real meaning. The real meaning is that when we receive the river, the Holy Ghost, he restores us to God, back to the image of God, the fellowship of God, communion with God the Father. We are never restored to communication with God until we get the Holy Ghost. No one can live the Christ life in its fullness until after he is sanctified and filled with the Holy Ghost, for it is the Holy Ghost that causes us to live the Christ life and walk in paths of righteousness.

Some years ago I had occasion to study the words "holy" and "righteousness." I give you the benefit of what I found. The words "holy" and "righteousness" are twin words. They go together throughout the Bible. "Righteous and holy." "Holy and righteous." The word "holy" refers to the inward life, a pure heart, perfect love, holiness imparted by the Holy Ghost, the cleansing blood, the inworking of the Spirit—holiness on the inside. The word "righteous" refers to the conduct, the outward life, right doing. Holiness refers to your inside living, righteousness refers to your outside living. When God sanctified Zacharias, the father of John the Baptist, Zacharias said, "I praise God that I can serve God in holiness and righteousness."

The next verse is one that has often been misunderstood and misquoted all through the ages. *Yea, though I walk through the valley of the shadow of death, I will fear no evil; for thou art with me; thy rod and thy staff they comfort me.* For hundreds of years nearly the whole church has taught that this means death. Millions and millions have read those words and have never discerned what they mean. In the first place, how did the man get in the valley of the shadow of death? Do you know? He did not get there by being sick or dying. He got there by walking in the paths of righteousness. It was not disease that got him there, but righteousness. The man did not die, because the next verse says he got out; and when he did get out, he had a banquet prepared right in the presence of his enemies. That shows the man did not die. If he had died, he would have gone to Heaven, and there are no enemies in Heaven. Do you see it?

Now let us find what that valley is. If you will notice the lives of all saints and patriarchs, you will find that after we receive the Holy Ghost and begin to live the sanctified life, Jesus Christ will lead us into a narrow place, a lonely place, a desert place, a sad place, a canyon. A canyon is a deep valley with perpendicular walls on either side. You do not have canyons here, but we have them in the Rocky Mountains. I have been in places where the walls were 2,000 feet high, and nothing there but desert, rock, and rattlesnakes. No one lived there and the sun went down at two o'clock in the afternoon. It is a land of shadows, a land of loneliness. That represents the path that Jesus leads a true bridehood saint. The saints of God in all generations have been led by God and the Shepherd to the Valley of the Shadow of Death without knowing where they were going. When sanctified people are led along this part of the journey, they do not know what ails them. They are sad, and they are lonely. They are tempted and tried. They live in a dry land. God is putting them to a test. God is proving their faith, so that they are separated from other people and drawn with a divine attraction to a narrow lovely place. Madame Guyon, Hester Ann Rogers, Mr. Fletcher, and other saints through all generations have known this. God weans the soul from the past, draws it where it can no more trust in Christian profession, or feelings, or lean on them. Here, you live a life of pure faith—a lonely life—a life where you are misunderstood and misrepresented, where it seems you have lost out. If you think that I am giving you a wrong sketch of the Scripture, I want to show you that Jesus Christ was led the same way. When Jesus was anointed with the Holy Ghost, he was taken along a lonely way. He was led out into the desert with rattlesnakes and wild beasts, no father or mother, no sister or brother, no one to cook his food. There alone, he went through the valley—the valley of the shadow of death.

It is a place of loneliness, of suffering, of testing, where one is stripped from his ambitions, his visions, where Jesus draws the soul to a life of perfect faith in his Word. Others do not know what is the matter; and if we dare tell anybody what we feel, we will not find one believer in a thousand who can sympathize with us, because most Christians live on their feelings. If one speaks of this experience to some preacher or evangelist who is not divinely illuminated, he does not understand, and says, "Well, Sister, or Brother, you are backslidden. You have lost out. Something is wrong. There is sin somewhere, and now you just go to the mourner's bench, and dig down and confess out." Some preachers do not know the deep things of God; and if the perplexed one falls into their hands, they will drag him to the altar and compel him to dig down and confess out. And when he gets to the altar, he feels like a fool. He may pray, and say, "Lord, I do not know what ails me! I love thee! I am all thine. I trust in thy blood. I am tired. I am sorely tempted; and if I dare to tell anybody how I feel, no one sympathizes with me. They think I am an old backslider, that I have lost out. But, Lord, when I search my heart, way down there, I know that I am thine. I know that my consecration is complete!" Madame Guyon spent five years in that valley, and she thought that she was lost. But she said, "If I am lost, I will do all I can to save souls while I live."

Now, then, how long will one stay in "the valley"? That depends on his knowledge, his faith, his prayers. In that place, the psalmist says, "Thy rod and thy staff they comfort me." What does that mean? God's rod is his Word, and in that lonely valley without any food or fire or friends, you have nothing in the world but a hard, dry walking stick. Now, see if I am right. Jesus spent forty days in the valley of the shadow of death, with wild beasts and rattlesnakes. He had nothing in the world but the Word of God to live on—no food, no fire, no bed. But he said there, "Thy rod and thy staff they comfort me." Jesus lived for forty days on the Book of the Second Blessing. I wonder if you know what book that is. It is the book of Deuteronomy. The word *detmos* means "second." The word *noma* means "experience." The word *exodus* means "go forth, get out from the world." When Jesus talked to the devil, and made quotations from the Bible, he did not quote from the book of Exodus, but from the book of Deuteronomy. Jesus lived forty days on the book of the Second Blessing, the second book. He ate, drank, and devoured the Word. He drew honey from the rod and the staff. Now, that is the way Christ leads us when we go through this lonely place. We are alone to feed on God's Word, to draw honey from the rock, to draw water from the rock. When you get there, you may read the book of Job. Nobody can fully understand the book of Job until he gets there. The higher critics do not know the book of Job. When you are going through the valley of the shadow of death, you will read Job and the Psalms. You will find words in these books that will make you say, "I declare those words fit my case." You will find your experience all told in those wonderful books. When you can draw honey from the rock, food and medicine from God's pure words, without leaning on your blessings, but live on the Word of God, then you will get out of the valley. That is the way Jesus got out, and that is the way you will get out. That forms a part of our discipline, our training, as we pass on from the experience of the new birth to the New Jerusalem. Jesus fed on the Word of God. When you feed on that, you will find comfort. Some of you have been through this lonely place. All of you will go through, if you will follow Jesus. You know when the iron mills make a piece of steel, after the steel is made, they put it in a hot furnace to be annealed, where it is tempered. It is good steel, but it must be annealed to get it where it will not have a flaw. And after God sanctifies his people, he puts them in the furnace to fit them for a heavenly kingdom.

Now take the next step: *"Thou preparest a table before me in the presence of mine enemies."* That shows that the man was not in Heaven, but on the earth, and in the presence of his enemies. These words were fulfilled directly in the life of Jesus after he went through the valley of the shadow of death. God sent his angels, and they found a dinner for him and spread the table on a rock in the wilderness. They prepared a table before Jesus right in the presence of the old devil. And the old green-eyed monster got behind the rocks and peeped out and saw the pure Jesus sitting on a rock, where the angels had got dinner for him. There the blessed Jesus had a glorious banquet with the angels, right in the presence of the devil.

Now, do you not see that those words were literally fulfilled? It was not a symbol. So Jesus prepares a banquet for us right in the presence of our enemies. After you get through the special testings and trials, if you go on and do not turn back, by and by Jesus, your Shepherd, will lead you beyond the valley, and he will give you a banquet beyond anything in your past life. There will come a fresh anointing upon your soul. I cannot describe it, but if you have received it, you know what I am talking about. There is a witness. There is a gentleness. There is a tenderness. There is a vast worldwide vision of God and Heaven.

Oh, the marvelous things God reveals to us after we go· through that dry place! God will give you the most wonderful enjoyment you ever had in your life. It is not that he will give you a new experience of sanctification, but he will wonderfully expand the sanctification you already have. He will widen, deepen, illuminate, and sweeten your experience. There will come a sweetness into your spirit. There will come a gentleness and compassion and a charity for all. You will get rid of all your sectarian harshness, your sectarian narrowness, your sanctified sectarianism and righteousness. You will get rid of your criticizing, harsh preaching, and severity with God's dear sheep.

Some time ago I attended a meeting in a certain holiness church. A woman evangelist was preaching there, whom I had known from her babyhood. I believe she was sanctified! But a great many sanctified folks are narrow and harsh and severe. They have not yet been through the valley of the shadow of death. That dear sister was lambasting the old saints. There were about two hundred people present, and most of them had been sanctified years before. When they did not come forward and fill the altar, she lambasted them, calling them old sticks, good for nothing but to warm their seats—and I sat there and felt like crying. Those dear old saints were starving for the Word of God. If they had been given a good meal, they would have been shouting happy.

O friends, I want to say that after God takes you through the valley of the shadow of death, and you are weaned from yourself and your past blessings, and you get out where you can rest on the Word of God alone, Jesus will give you a banquet! You will get insight into God and Scriptures. You will have an enlarged life of prayer, of faith, of compassion. You will make allowance for people. There is a wideness, there is a tenderness, there is a sweetness, there is a heavenliness that will come down upon your soul away beyond what you experienced when you were first sanctified. It is not sanctification, but is a growth of the sanctification that God has given you. You will have a banquet in the presence of your enemies—the people that criticize you, despise you, denounce you, misunderstand you, will not pay you the money they owe you. Oh, how God will bless your soul! God will be your Friend. He will justify you. He will put his arms around you and comfort you in the presence of your foes, and will rebuke the devourer for your sake. Do you see it? There is a banquet for us. Blessed be his name!

When you start from Illinois for southern California, you leave the green pastures of Illinois, cross the river, go down the deep canyons to the Rocky Mountains, and cross those great, dry deserts. That is a part of your journey. You must go that way. When you get near southern California, you leave the narrow canyons of Colorado, with the rattlesnakes, and run up across the Sierra Mountains, and there you behold the glory land. For one hundred miles, you see roses, lilies, orange groves, lemon groves, and fruits of all kinds. It is a place where the sun shines almost continually, and where there is everlasting summer. You have left the deserts, and reach southern California, the most glorious place in all the world. (So many of us think.) This is an illustration of how a soul is led into the depths of the riches of God's grace. It is a picture of God's revelation of how Jesus leads a sanctified soul into strength and power from on high.

"Thou anointest my head with oil." David says, "I shall be anointed with fresh oil." When Samuel poured the oil on the head of young David, they were at the dinner table. Samuel was told to sit down, but he said, "I cannot eat your dinner until I anoint one of your sons." Seven sons passed in succession before Samuel, and then, the eighth one, David, was brought. His seven brothers were his enemies. You will find that afterwards they criticized him, found fault with him. But right there in the

presence of his enemies, at the dinner table, the prophet anointed him with fresh oil.

"Thou anointest my head with oil, my cup runneth over." Did you ever get the runover blessing—the overflow? If you will follow the Shepherd, you will get to the place where your cup will run over. There will be a wideness in your prayers. There will be a liberality in your giving of your money and your time and your thoughts. Your soul will expand to take in the entire world. For years and years, I have carried the whole world in my soul. I remember all nations and tongues and people. I remember the work in Africa. I pray for the work in South America and the west Indies. I pray for India, China, Korea, and Japan, and for missionaries in all parts of the world. Oftentimes I weep and pray for the poor lost heathen. O friends, God has widened my soul! I do not have many demonstrations. I am not built on that line. I enjoy demonstrations, and I enjoy the shouting and the leaping and the dancing in the Holy Spirit. There is something in my soul that responds to these chords of music—the laughter of the holiness people, the songs of the sanctified—my soul gets happy. I thank God that my cup runs over, and I want to do all I can for the lost.

"Surely goodness and mercy shall follow me all the days of my life." "Surely goodness and mercy." Goodness is one angel, and mercy is another angel. These two angels are our guardians. That shows that the man did not die in the canyon. He got out, and goodness and mercy, like two guardian angels, guide him all the days of his life. In the end, he shall dwell in the house of the Lord, the New Jerusalem. Before Dean Alford, a marvelous scholar and Bible teacher on the second coming of Christ, died, he said he wanted on his tombstone: "The lodge of a pilgrim on his way to the New Jerusalem." Friends, this Psalm is a perfect revelation of the experience of a soul following Jesus through this life, up into the home of everlasting life. Amen!

CHAPTER 19

The Divine Face

THE human face is the most consummate and exquisite stroke of creative thought yet revealed. Even if God should produce a finer thing, it would be impossible for us to appreciate it. It is the culmination of material grandeur and beauty, the focus where all the rays of creation's glory are collected, blended, and irradiated.

The apostle tells us that the glory of the Godhead beamed from the face of Jesus Christ. Oh, what a tender, beautiful, and overpowering condescension—that the living blazes of infinite majesty should so shade themselves beneath the tiny and subtle features of human clay! There are some very interesting thoughts and suggestions connected with the human countenance, and these suggestions are heightened and beautified in contemplating Christ as the face of Divinity. Though the human face is so exceedingly diminutive when compared to other forms of creation, yet it contains more significance within the compass of a few little inches than the magnificent area of a vast continent. The continent may have waving forests for hair, lofty plateaus for a forehead, and mountain range for a nose, sparkling lakes for eyes, trickling streams for tears, flowery landscapes for cheeks, caves for ears, canyons for lips, the peninsula of Florida for a chin, or Niagara for a tongue; but all this stupendous range of territory, with its variegated glories, is thrown into the shade by that minute piece of divine art which reposes on a mother's breast.

The human face is God's volume of creation written in shorthand. And Christ brings to us in the narrow dimensions of man's countenance all those traits of supreme emotion and thought which can be unveiled. There are more ideas and feelings bursting from the face of Jesus than from all the charming and elaborate forms of the universe besides.

The face is the most intelligible piece of mechanism in creation. It takes poets and philosophers months and years to decipher the mystic language of the stars, oceans, and mountains; but in less than a minute, a little six-month-old will read more in the parent's hovering visage than you could spread out on the Atlantic in a century. Oh, what a facile spelling book is formed with their lightning pages of eyes and lips! A curl in the cheek pronounces a gulf of sentiment. Infant and sage, man and brute, catch the meaning of those wonderful looks.

And so Jesus is the easiest volume of theology to read yet published. Men may pore over tomes of theological lore, and that is right. Poets may sing of seeing God in clouds and hearing him in the wind, and that is right; but it takes time to spell the music. When Peter caught the electric flash of Christ's eye in the judgment hall, it required only a few twinkling seconds to interpret an ocean of blended pity and rebuke. The expiring whisper of Jesus exhales a sweeter and more intelligible music than all the silver-tongued choiring constellations. One indignant frown shed from his majestic brow will spread a quicker consternation among the beholders than a hundred scowling storms.

While the philosopher is reading God's benignity in a summer landscape, the tear-washed eye of faith surveys the loveliness of a million summers in the approving smile of Christ. He who travels up to the divine bosom on the stairway of material nature has a long and circuitous journey; the open face of Messiah is the soul's shortest and softest path to the interior paradise of the infinite. No dumb enigma is there. On the face of nature we see God's thoughts in translation.

In the face of Jesus, we see God himself in our own fond and native dialect. The human face is a bridge from the material to the spiritual. Here spirit and matter hold the most intimate fellowship. So deeply is the countenance saturated with the ethereal streams of mind, that we scarcely associate it with material things. It is the transparent medium through which gleams the shape and complexion of the mighty soul, the sweet and harmonious marriage of mind and matter. Through the facial organs, as through a royal archway, the soul passes out upon the panorama of creation, and the lineaments of creation crowd into the chambers of the soul.

This, also, is eminently applicable to Christ. The lovely face of the meek Nazarene not only spans the void between the spiritual and the material, but the still broader chasm between the Deity and the lowliest of his creatures. Through that form, God has espoused himself to all material worlds and beings. That face wasn't assumed as a delicate mask in which God was to play some brilliant part in the drama of immortal history, and then abandon it forever, but as the everlasting enshrinement from which will blaze the unsullied luster of divine manifestations. What rapt and elevated pleasures will it afford, to have a visible contemplation of that reconciled and transfigured countenance! John saw his hair like wool, white as snow, and eyes like a flame of fire. There will be such virtue in the survey that the thought of sin will be swept from every faculty.

> There we shall see his face
> And never, never sin;
> There from the rivers of his grace,
> Drink endless pleasures in!

CHAPTER 20

Isaiah's Vision of America

Written during the World War

THERE is clear and infallible proof that the Holy Spirit gave to the prophet Isaiah a vision of America as existing and playing a conspicuous part in the providence of God among the nations of the earth in the last days. In the very nature of things it is reasonable to suppose that a nation of the magnitude and power and service of the United States should occupy a place in divine prophecy. When we consider the origin of this nation, and its being born of religious principle, and the work it has done in the providence of God, and the work it has yet to perform, we need not be surprised to find that these things were foretold by the Holy Spirit in connection with the prophecies upon other nations of the earth. I want to call your attention to the following striking points in connection with this prophecy:

The prophet Isaiah was led to deliver a series of prophecies concerning various nations as to events that transpire in the last days. In chapter thirteen he delivers a prophecy concerning Babylon on the east. In chapter fifteen he delivers a prophecy concerning Moab on the southeast of Jerusalem. Then in chapter seventeen he delivers a prophecy concerning Damascus, and in chapter nineteen another prophecy concerning Egypt. Following that in chapter twenty-one is a prophecy about Media, and in chapter twenty-three a prophecy concerning Tyre, making, as it were, a circle of nations. Right in the midst of this circle, in chapter eighteen, he delivers a prophecy concerning a country which at that time had no name. Now it is evident that this prophecy in chapter eighteen forms a part of this great message concerning the nations of the earth in the last days. Let me call your attention to the marvelous items mentioned in this chapter and see how infallibly they refer to our American nation.

Where we read, "Woe to the land shadowing with wings," the word "Woe" is incorrect and should be "Ho," for it is an exclamation of surprise or of admiration, and not a term of condemnation. In the prophet's vision he saw a nation arise far in the west, of wonderful power and service, but which had no name. He called it, "The land of outstretched wings," which is a more correct translation than in the Authorized Version. It was by divine providence that the eagle was selected as the emblem of the United States as a nation, but there was a deeper truth hidden under the emblem, and that was that America should be, in the providence of God, a land that should serve as a refuge to all other nations on the earth. It was to have a government for the protection of all other people, a land of religious liberty and freedom of conscience, a land that would welcome to its shores the downtrodden and the suffering people scattered abroad upon the face of the earth. It is a singular fact that this term of being "a land of outstretched wings" for the shelter of all other people cannot be applied to any other country on the face of the earth. Since the world began, there never has been any other country that from its beginning offered a welcome and a hospitality to all other people for the purpose of giving them religious and civil liberty except America. When the leading French statesman made his address of welcome to President Wilson in the city of Paris, he spoke of Mr. Wilson being "the representative of that nation that stretched its wings abroad for the protection and deliverance of Europe," and he unwittingly used the very words that Isaiah used twenty-six hundred years ago, probably knowing nothing of Isaiah's prophecy. So accurate was the fulfillment of prophecy that he used the words of the infallible inspiration.

The prophet speaks of this land as lying beyond, that is, west of the rivers of Ethiopia, or Africa. What country is it that lies west of Africa or Ethiopia except America? If you stand in the city of Jerusalem, where Isaiah prophesied, and look due west, you will see no country until your vision strikes the coast of South Carolina and Georgia, which is due west from Jerusalem. This proves infallibly that the prophecy was not spoken to Africa, but to a nation that was west of Africa; and it proves he was not speaking to any country in Asia or in Europe. Hence, the words can apply to no other land on earth except the United States.

The prophet speaks of this land as one "that sendeth ambassadors by the sea" in vessels upon the waters. The word "ambassadors" means men who travel on business for the government—not those who travel for pleasure, but those sent by government authority. Here is a prophecy about America which was never fulfilled until 1917 and 1918 when America sent over two million people "in swift ships" across the Atlantic on business for the government, to defeat an ambitious tyrant and liberate and protect other nations. It is true that in all generations people have traveled in ships, and nations have sent their soldiers at various times across the sea. But never since the world was made has any nation sent over two million people across the ocean on government business, to fight for the liberty and welfare of mankind. And hence this prophecy cannot be applied to any other country on earth but America and her action in the late war against Germany.

"To a nation scattered and peeled." It should read, "From a nation tall and clean shaven." The new version renders it "tall and polished." It is evident that the prophet had a vision of a vast army of men like trees with the bark peeled off, and the translation should be, "a nation tall and clean shaven." In the late war America raised and equipped over three million soldiers at home or abroad, and those soldiers averaged the tallest of any similar army ever marshaled on the earth. The American soldiers in the late war averaged five feet eleven inches in height, being the tallest army in size the world has ever seen. And then, only think of it! Of these three million soldiers not a single man wore a beard. Though many had a mustache, not one wore a beard. Here is another item that cannot be applied to any army that has ever existed in the past generations. Here is a fact that God foresaw twenty-six centuries ago, and had it put down in the Holy Scriptures. For it was a fact so noticeable, as compared with all other armies, as to make it worthy of record; and it forms an infallible proof that the reference could only be made to the army of Americans.

"To a people terrible from their beginning." Here is another remarkable statement which cannot be applied to any other nation that has ever existed except the United States. Suppose an infant should whip its mother the day it was born, would not that infant appropriately bear the name of being terrible? Such was the case with this American nation; for when it was first born it conquered the largest and most powerful nation which at that time existed in the world. This is a historical fact which cannot be applied to any other nation on the globe; for while other nations in their history have gradually acquired a great strength and power and become terrible in some respects, yet no other nation has ever existed that from its beginning manifested an unconquerable power except the United States. Hence there is an expression in prophecy which it is impossible to apply to any other country or people.

It is added by the prophet that this character of being terrible or powerful is to continue down to the end. The expression in the Scripture is "a people terrible from their beginning hitherto," which the new version has rendered "from the beginning and onward," but the original word signifies "onward to the end." Here we have an infallible prophecy that America will never be conquered down to the end of the age. This is not because of the goodness of America, but because of God's plan concerning the nation; and these infallible words of prophecy will surely be fulfilled.

"A nation meted out and trodden down." The literal translation would be, "a land measured out under the treading," that is, a land measured out under feet. Here is another startling prophecy that nobody on earth could have foreseen except the infinite mind of God. About the time that Ohio and Florida were taken into the Union as states or territories, the government passed a law that all public lands should be surveyed by the North Star and cut up into mile square sections, and these sections subdivided into quarter sections of half a mile square, which is the amount allotted for a homestead by the government. Now just look at it: Up to that time, in all the countries on earth where surveys of land had been made, the portions of land were divided by some local boundaries, beginning at some rock, or tree, or river, or mountain, or ocean shore; and the portions of land were described by these local boundaries, as we find was the case in dividing up the land of Canaan under Joshua. The American government was the first in the history of the human race to divide or survey the land by measurements according to ranges with the North Star. All the land in America from the western edge of Pennsylvania to the Pacific Ocean and from Canada to Mexico has been surveyed by lines of measurement staked off in sections and quarter sections, as also the state of Florida, which was admitted into the Union about 1845 after the law of general surveys had been passed. There are millions of people in America who do not know of this fact of the government dividing and surveying the land in sections with lines pointed due north and south and east and west, but the Holy Spirit showed that to the prophet Isaiah twenty-six hundred years ago.

"Whose land the rivers have spoiled." This is an incorrect translation and should be, "a land divided by rivers." If you will look at the map of the United States, you will notice that it is divided north and south by the great Mississippi River, from Canada to the Gulf, and then divided east and west by the Ohio, the Tennessee, the Missouri, the Arkansas and the Columbia; and these great rivers cut the country into sections north and south and east and west. You cannot find any other country on the globe that is divided in this way, in great sections east, west, north, and south, by rivers, and hence this is a prophetic word which cannot be applied to any other country but America.

Now comes a prophetic word more startling than any of the preceding: "All ye inhabitants of the world, and dwellers on the earth, see ye, when he lifteth up an ensign on the mountains; and when he bloweth a trumpet, hear ye." This part of the prophecy was never fulfilled until 1918, at the time that our president began to deliver his messages concerning the principles connected with the great Peace Conference, and with the conditions that should be complied with by the nations of the earth in forming the League of Nations, or in coming to some understanding with regard to the adjustment of nations and governments with each other. Ignoring all politics and all personalities, the prophet saw that the head of this American nation should be the one in the providence of God to dictate the terms for the forming of worldwide agreements among the nations. Such a thing has never before happened since the world was made. Empires have risen and fallen, thousands of battles have been fought, and human governments and nations have passed through all sorts of experiences in war and in peace; but in these last days the conditions of the world and human governments are of such a character that God has in a mysterious way compelled the American nation, through its chosen rulers, to be at the head of all the nations of the world, and to take the leadership in dictating terms and regulations for the management of human governments, and the adjusting of different claims, and the settlement of national rights and privileges. Here is proof of an infinite mind and an infallible vision that all nations are to heed the words of America.

These words have been quietly reposing in the pages of God's infallible Book for twenty-six long centuries, and not until a few days ago were they brought out of their quiet resting place and accomplished as a literal, stupendous fact before the people of the world. God said that this nation "should lift up an ensign on the mountains," and "blow a trumpet." The lifting up of a flag and blowing of a trumpet certainly means the declaration of war. When such things take place by this "nation of outstretched wings," then all the inhabitants of the world and all the dwellers on the earth are commanded "to hear," to give heed to what this nation says and does. The fulfillment of this Scripture by what has transpired in the late war, and through the various addresses of the American presidents, is so perfect a fulfillment of prophecy that it is impossible to misconstrue it or apply it to any other nation.

"In that time shall the present be brought unto the Lord of hosts from a people tall and clean shaven." This word "present," or "gift," is in the original a generic term and includes all sorts and all sizes of gifts and presents. Now look at the facts in the case. Since the great European war began, this American nation has sent to many nations gifts and presents of everything that can be mentioned. The American nation has sent wheat, corn, meats, all kinds of foodstuffs, clothing, ammunition, medicine, railroad material, timber, nurses, surgeons, soldiers, ministers, artists, laborers, and cash money, not only by the millions, but by the hundreds of millions, to help the needy nations in Europe as well as in Western Asia. Such a thing has never occurred in the whole history of the human race before. All the gifts that other nations have ever made to their fellow nations have been but a drop in the bucket compared with the numerous gifts that have gone over from America to the European nations. The sending of relief in foodstuffs, medicine, munitions of war, and all kinds of benevolences and donations has been of a magnitude that startles the wildest imagination, and surpasses anything that could have been dreamed of a few years ago. On top of all these multiplied gifts, when the American president cabled from France that the American nation should supply a hundred million dollars to take care of the poor and distressed among the nations, it was readily acceded to by the American government. There is no parallel to this in the history of the world. The Almighty God saw this and showed it to the prophet Isaiah, and he put it down in the infallible Bible; and we stand amazed when we read these words in connection with their fulfillment, which is so exact and literal that it cannot be misunderstood.

The prophecy is concluded, as we might expect it would be, with a reference to the Jew. The last line in the prophecy is that this American nation is to help the Jew, for it speaks of sending things and help to the place of the "name of the Lord of hosts at Mt. Zion." Zion always refers to Israel or the Jew. The Jew is God's key to human history, and Moses tells us in chapter thirty-three of Deuteronomy that God deals with all nations as they are related to the people of Israel. Palestine has been rescued from the Turk, rescued forever from that unspeakable monster, and will evidently soon become the homeland of a Jewish government. According to God's Word, America is to take an active interest either in the formation or in the preservation of that Jewish state.

There must be a special mission in God's providence for the American nation to perform in the history of the world. All the great crisis events in the Bible seem to have occurred in the month of April. It is more than likely that God made Adam and Eve in the month of April and that Noah's flood occurred in the month of April; for the dove, when she went forth from the ark, was hunting for leaves to build her nest, indicative of the spring of the year. We know the Hebrews left Egypt at the Passover, which was in April. They also crossed the Jordan about the same time, that is, in April, because at that time the spring floods were on. It is evident that Jesus was born in the month of April, and not in December when it was too cold for the shepherds to be out at night. We know that Christ was crucified in the month of April, at the time of Easter. All the Scriptures that speak of Christ's second coming seem to indicate that he will come in the month of April, for Christ refers to the time as being the spring of the year, when summer is nigh; and Solomon speaks of the time as being when the winter is past and gone and the flowers appear and the birds are singing. Now, it is a singular thing in providence that every crisis in the history of America has occurred in the month of April, for all the wars that this country has ever had began in the month of April. These things could not possibly be accidental. There is an infinite providence in relation to America so remarkable that it ought to awaken in the minds of the American people to the dealings of God, and lead us as a people to recognize and worship and trust in that infinite uler of all worlds, because he whose eye is spread abroad all over the nations takes notice of each one of us, and has a plan and a purpose in our lives. The prophet tells us that God's dealings with mankind are the same whether he deals with a nation or with one man only.

CHAPTER 21

Holy Courage

HOLY courage is not the sort of courage that men are most acquainted with. It is what the world most needs, and yet it is what the world and worldly churchmen most criticize and hate. The world hates most what it needs most. Holy courage is a perpetual and burning condemnation of all manner of ungodliness. It is not an earth-born nor brain-born. It is a celestial species of experience and character. Holy courage blooms only on the stern of an utterly pure conscience. It blossoms only under the noonday of spiritual light in the soul. He who has the consciousness of an unfettered holy courage in his inmost soul knows to a good degree what are the emotions of an angel. But holy courage is enthroned in the heart and will only when self has been utterly crucified—only when the love of fame and power and place and ease, mental pride, and ecclesiastical pride, and all physical and spiritual impurity is washed away—only then does holy courage wrap the soul with unflinching bravery. People always praise this holy courage when it does not come too close to them. Those who have yet the remains of the carnal mind admire this courage like they do a volcano—at a handsome distance.

There is as deep a need for unflinching holy boldness today as ever. Holy courage is as much needed in the pulpit as ever. It is not the gift of the church. It does not fall from ordaining hands. It does not spring from strong nerves, nor from the stimulus of strong coffee or tobacco. It is not the product of culture, politics, or military life. This holy courage comes of conscious purity and the filling baptism of the Holy Ghost.

A minister may be brave enough to aspire after the high places, brave enough to denounce Huxley and Boss Tweed, and yet he may not have the serene bravery of God and the holy angels in his soul.

He may be conscious all the time (although too proud to own it) that his soul is internally fettered. The people in the pew may see, as plain as day, that spiritual cowardice still lingers somewhere under the orator's ribs. The world and the visible church both need messengers of God so perfectly purged, and filled of the Spirit, as not to fear rich and cultured sinners, who are not ever afraid of offending someone, who have no fear about their salaries or the votes of the conference, who are not afraid to preach very simple Bible sermons, who are not afraid of telling their experience, who are not in the least afraid of the flattery or abuse of the whole world, who so bury themselves in the bosom of God that the created universe cannot scare them, who so fix their eyes on Jesus, that they are oblivious to stained glass, pipe organs, fine clothes, and the foolish whims of proud and theater-going church members, who walk so close with God that, when they preach, the people will feel as if a solemn section of eternity was falling on them. But this holy courage cannot be studied out, nor thought out, nor volitioned out, nor counterfeited. It comes only into an utterly purified heart, and is one of the fruits of perfect love.

Chapter 22

Others May, You Cannot

IF God has called you to be really like Christ, he will draw you into a life of crucifixion and humility, and put on you such demands of obedience that he will not allow you to follow other Christians; and in many ways he will seem to let other good people do things which he will not let you do.

Other Christians and ministers who seem very religious and useful may push themselves, pull wires, and work schemes to carry out their plans; but you cannot do it. If you attempt it, you will meet with such failure and rebuke from the Lord as to make you sorely penitent.

Others may boast of themselves, of their work, of their success, of their writings, but the Holy Spirit will not allow you to do any such thing; and if you begin it, he will lead you into some deep mortification that will make you despise yourself and all your good works.

Others will be allowed to succeed in making money, or having a legacy left to them, or in having luxuries; but it is likely God will keep you poor, because he wants you to have something far better than gold, and that is a helpless dependence on him, that he may have the privilege of supplying your needs day by day out of an unseen treasury.

The Lord will let others be honored, and put forward, and keep you hid away in obscurity, because he wants to produce some choice fragrant fruit for his coming glory which can only be produced in the shade.

He will let others be great, but keep you small. He will let others do a work for him, and get the credit for it, but he will make you work and toil on without knowing how much you are doing. Then, to make your work still more precious, he will let others get the credit for the work which you have done; and this will make your reward ten times greater when Christ comes.

The Holy Spirit will put a strict watch over you, with a jealous love, and will rebuke you for little words and feelings, or for wasting your time, which other Christians never seem distressed over. So make up your mind that God is an infinite Sovereign, and has a right to do as he pleases with his own. He will not explain to you a thousand things which may puzzle your reason in his, dealings with you. He will take you at your word. If you absolutely sell yourself to be his love slave, he will wrap you up in a jealous love and let other people say and do many things that you cannot do or say.

Settle it forever, then, that you are to deal directly with the Lord Jesus, and that he is to have the privilege of tying your tongue, or chaining your hand, or closing your eyes, in ways that he does not deal with others. Now, when you are so possessed with the living God that you are, in your secret heart, pleased and delighted over this peculiar, personal, private, jealous guardianship and management of the Lord Jesus over your life, you will have found the vestibule of Heaven.

"What things were gain to me, those I counted loss for Christ" (Philippians 3:7).

CHAPTER 23

A Visit to Uncle Jack

DURING our recent visit to St. Augustine, Florida, we sought out the curiosities to be seen—the ancient Spanish mansions, built of coquina stones, the old Spanish fort and cathedral, the antique city gates, the military graves where lie the heroes of the Indian wars, the Ball Place, and last but by no means least, the old colored saint whom hundreds of Northern people visit every winter as one of the outstanding curiosities of the place. Doubtless the old patriarch often gets weary of being an exhibition in his little cabin nearly every day for four or five months. Many of his visitors are poor worldlings or, if Christians, they do not definitely make it known to him. But when his guests make it known that they are positively religious, it is the joy of the old man's soul to enter into religious conversation with them. Uncle Jack lives alone in a cabin and has a half-acre of ground filled with orange trees, enclosed in one of the most beautiful estates in Florida known as the Ball Place.

Uncle Jack was formerly the slave of Buckingham Smith, who purchased him on his arrival from Africa eighty years ago, when he was about fifteen years old, so that he is now between ninety and ninety-five years of age. As a reward for his faithfulness, his old master willed him this cabin and half acre during his natural life. The beautiful grounds all around him have been sold and have changed owners, but this old ebony heir of God still holds undisputed sway in his little domain. As our party entered his little dingy abode, Brother Leonard saluted him; and we soon fell into religious talk and reminiscences of bygone years. He said when he was six or seven years old his tribe in Africa was at war with another tribe, and that he was captured and sold to an

African master. Later he was bought and sold several times, and when about fifteen years old was brought over in a slave ship to Florida. He gave us some incidents of his slave life.

He was a very trusted servant, was for many years his master's treasurer, kept watch over his money, paid his master's bills, and always took a receipt for the pay. His young mistress married a surgeon who went to the Mexican War. The young mistress, with her little babe, had to go to New York. They could not travel so far then without a servant; but New York was a free state, and the difficulty was to find a slave that would tread free soil and voluntarily return to his owner. Uncle jack was picked out for this emergency. Some said, "You will never see Jack again!" But his old mistress charged him to take good care of Mary and the baby on the ship, and not let the abolitionists get hold of him, but to come back or else she would "fret herself to death." (I have been told of some cases where slaveowners did actually fret themselves to death.) Jack was urged by his colored friends in New York to stay there, but he took the first vessel homeward. When he landed at St. Augustine his old mistress got up from a sickbed and walked halfway to the wharf to meet him with tears of joy.

Uncle Jack is a member of the Methodist Episcopal Church; and when we told him that two of us were Methodist preachers and the other a class leader, he seemed in his proper element. And when I said, "Uncle Jack, shall we sing for you?" he burst into weeping and, placing his wrinkled hands over his eyes, said, "Thank God, thank God! He so good. He send kind white friends to sing for poor old Jack!" After we had sung a few hymns, the old man said, "Let's pray." We all knelt; and with tremulous voice and streaming eyes, he led us in prayer, which I wish I could report. It was short, pathetic, orthodox, and closed with the Lord's Prayer. His language was a strange, almost unreportable one, being English words thrown into his native idiom and uttered with a short, quick accent. He said he was first convicted of sin out in the field by hearing a voice say over and over, "You die now, you never go where holy angels are today." This is a sample of his idiom. He said so impressively, "When man speak, we trifle. But when God speak, we can't trifle. His voice like thunder. He speak to the heart. His voice make soul tremble. Can't trifle with God." He said that he tried a long time to learn the Lord's Prayer. He heard his mistress teach it to the children, and for days would go around repeating fragments of it, but said his head was too thick to learn. But one night, in a dream, God sent him a beautiful little boy to teach him the Lord's Prayer. Next morning he knew every word and has not forgotten it since. He said, "Man learning we forget, but what God tell us we never forget."

For many years he was a local preacher, and he still kept his license in a box under his bed. He told us how the power of the Spirit used to fall on the people in his meetings, and whites and blacks would cry and scream under convicting power. In those days he had much persecution for his noisy meetings. But those times are past. He is now honored of all, and calmly waits that chariot which will move him from the shade and odors of his orange trees to the sweeter groves of the Paradise of God.

CHAPTER 24

Ode

THE following lines were written impromptu on the occasion of the Semi-centennial celebration on Ennall's Spring Camp Ground, Maryland, August 18, 1869, by Rev. George Douglas Watson. A suitable tune was immediately composed by Professor Fischer of Philadelphia, who was also present. The chorus, we believe, was added by Rev. Alfred Cookman, and has become immensely popular in all our social meetings.

> The years are rolling past
>   The future's dawning fast
> And wider spreads thy reign
>   O holy Lamb once slain.
>
> Chorus:
> Still we're trusting, Lord, in thee,
>   Dear Lamb of Calvary.
> Still we're trusting, Lord, in thee,
>   Dear Lamb of Calvary!
>
> On this prayer-honored ground
>   How many hearts have found
> The priceless boon of love
>   Who reign with Christ above.
>
> At this half century year,
>   Let saints and angels share
> Our joy in him we love
>   Who through the ages move.

153

Now, holy Lord, come down
Place on this year a crown,
Approving what is done
And lead us safely on!

"I will cleanse them from all their iniquity."

Jesus My All

My heart sings a song from morning till night,
A song full of liberty, love, and of light,
A song of the Canaan land full of delight,
   And all of my song is Jesus.

My heart is at rest from sin and from fear,
A rest from all doubting, disappointment, and care,
A rest like the sky, bending calm o'er the year
   And all my rest is Jesus.

My heart hath a gift with value untold,
A gift of unbounded peace, richer than gold,
A gift that the universe cannot all hold
   And all of my gift is Jesus.

My heart hath a light in the cloudiest day,
A light which illumines each moment my way,
A light which will not let the little one stray,
And all of my light is Jesus.

My heart hath a friend who talks nothing but love,
And his speech falls as soft as starlight above
A friend that abideth and will not remove,
And that dearest friend is Jesus.

My heart hath a home and it wanders no more,
A home like to that on that glorified shore,
A home where all goodness embosoms its store
And all of my home is Jesus.

To obtain additional copies of this book, and to see a list of
other great Christian titles, including more by
G. D. Watson, visit our web site:
www.KingsleyPress.com

www.ingramcontent.com/pod-product-compliance
Lightning Source LLC
Chambersburg PA
CBHW060758050426
42449CB00008B/1447